Psilocybin Mushrooms

Everything You Need to Know About Magic Mushrooms From History to Medical Perspective. A Real Guide to Cultivation and Safe Use

JONATHAN SYRIAN

Table of Contents

CHAPTER ONE

Introduction to Mushrooms

Mushrooms have been a part of the human diet for centuries. They have been a part of meals even before their proper discovery. People have been using them in their special meals and medicines, but they didn't know the actual name of it. Mushroom and its use as edibles by humans have a long history. With the development in food style, the style of using mushrooms was also changed.

Humans are familiar with mushrooms long before the use of microorganisms. Mushroom is a fungus, and a proper definition of it was presented by Chang and Miles, where they said that a mushroom is a macro fungus which has a distinctive fruiting body, either epigeous or hypogenous, which is sizeable enough to be seen with the eye and picked by hand. They were not only used in Europe but also in the early Roman Empire, in Middle America, South America, and in Asia as part of special meals. Before the cultivation of mushrooms by man, they were found in the sediments of Lakes in Germany, Switzerland, and Austria. People didn't know anything about those umbrella-shaped puffballs found in moist places in prehistoric times. In ancient Greece and Rome, the toughest and hardest mushrooms like truffle and orange were the most expensive mushrooms.

Mushroom Usage in Prehistoric Times

Prehistoric times had evidence of mushroom usage in meals and medicines, but the exact time and place of its discovery are not clear. The Saharan aboriginal tribes of North Africa were possibly using mushrooms, as their stone painting showed, which were carved around 9000BC. In Spain, similar paintings were discovered, carved 6000 years ago. This evidence showed that some mushrooms were used in some specific rituals, and they were part of cultural meals as well. As per Egyptian culture and history of mushrooms, Egyptians considered mushrooms as "plants of immortality." Egyptian Pharaohs seemed interested in mushrooms so much that they announced and proclaimed that it is a special fruit meant only for gods. Therefore, in Egypt during the reign of Pharaohs, mushroom was considered an essential part of royalty meals.

Other civilizations of the world also considered mushrooms as something having superpowers. In Russia, China, Latin America, Mexico and Greece, mushroom was an essential part of some of their rituals. At some point, people thought that eating mushrooms could produce superhuman powers, and can lead a person on a path towards the gods.

History of Mushroom Cultivation

The cultivation of mushrooms was started back in 600s, in Asia. But in Europe, the fungus (mushroom) cultivation was started in the 1600s. History shows that the cultivation of mushrooms in Paris was started in the 1650s when a native farmer saw growing fungus in his field of melons. He then thought to cultivate this fungus on a commercial level, and this was the time to change thoughts about mushrooms. He delivered this umbrella-shaped fungus to restaurants where it was used as a dish. That type of mushrooms was named "Parisian Mushroom."

Researchers found fungus growing in caves around Paris, whose history dates back in the 1600s when French gardeners found that the humid and cool environment of caves is suitable for mushroom cultivation. Therefore mushrooms were cultivated at large scale in caves. In the Netherlands, mushrooms were introduced for cultivation in the 1800s but in small scales. Then after some time, large scale cultivation of mushrooms was done in marl mines in Limburg. After caves and mines, other methods of mushroom cultivation were developed, which then resulted in high mushroom yields in the region. Before that, mushrooms were specific, and they were only available for elites. Dutch people had the strictest rules and controls for mushroom cultivation. This was the reason the Netherlands became the largest mushroom producing country 50 years ago. However, China and the USA joined the competition of mushroom cultivation. China produces about 70% of the world's mushrooms now, so China is at the first position in mushroom cultivation, and then comes the USA and Netherlands.

Types and Classification of Mushrooms

Types of Mushrooms

In general, mushrooms are divided into four categories including, Edible mushrooms, Medicine or therapeutic mushrooms, Poisonous mushrooms, and Miscellaneous (mix) mushrooms.

Edible mushrooms: These mushrooms can be used in the human diet. They have been a part of meals for centuries in different civilizations. Some examples of these mushrooms are Cantharellus cibarius, Hericium erinaceus, Boletus edulis, etc.

Medicinal or Therapeutic mushrooms

Hundreds of mushroom species have therapeutic and healing properties, and therefore many of them are used in medicines. Some mushrooms having hallucinogenic properties are also considered as natural healers. For example, an old healer from Mexico, Maria Sabina, used hallucinogenic Psilocybin mushrooms to heal mental, spiritual, and physical problems. Examples of some therapeutic mushrooms are Fomitopsis pinicola, Hericium erinaceus, inonotus obliquus, etc.

Poisonous Mushrooms: They are extremely poisonous, which can even lead to death. In the next section, there is a detailed discussion about poisonous mushrooms. An example of such poisonous mushrooms is Amanita phalloides.

Miscellaneous mushrooms: There is a large number of mushrooms whose features and special characteristics are yet to be discovered.

Classification of Mushrooms

As mentioned earlier, mushrooms belong to Fungi, which was a part of kingdom plantae first. But due to its distinct properties, different from animals and plants and thousands of species, Fungi was named as a separated kingdom. So, we can say that mushrooms belong to kingdom "Fungi." Like other fungi, mushrooms don't contain chlorophyll and are heterotrophic. They can't make their own food; therefore, they extract food from other organisms and their environment. Two of the several phyla of Kingdom Fungi are *Basidiomycota* and *Ascomycota.* Most of the mushroom species belong to these phyla. Five main phyla of Kingdom Fungi and their point of recognition are:

Phyla	***Characteristics***
Ascomycota	Mostly sac fungi, like yeast, etc.
Basidiomycota	Macro fungi, can be picked by hand, like puffballs, mushrooms, bracket fungi, etc.
Zygomycota	Molds, mycorrhizal fungus, filamentous fungi, decomposers
Chytridiomycota	Primitive fungi, chytrids
Deuteromycota	Fungi whose mode of reproduction is asexual reproduction

Table 1.1: Main phyla of fungi

Mushrooms are not limited to edible mushrooms. There is a number of mushrooms having different properties and specifications. Mushrooms are edible, but some are poisonous, and have hallucinogenic properties. Mushrooms are actually fruiting bodies of fungi that belong to the class Basidiomycetes and order Agaricales, which belong to the Phylum Basidiomycota. The following table shows a simple classification of mushrooms for understanding:

Class	**Order**	**Genus**	**Example**

Basidiomycetes	Agaricales	*Agaricus*	*Agaricus campestris*
Agaricomycetes	Cantharellales	*Cantharellus*	*Cantharellus cibarius*
Agaricomycetes	Rassulales	*Lentinellus*	*Lentinellus cochleatus*
Agaricomycetes	Polyporales	*Lentinus*	*Daedaleopsis confragosa*

Table 1.2: Popular classes of Fungi and their orders with example species

The order Agaricales has about 30 families with 250 genera and 10,000 species. They are also called "Gilled mushrooms" because these mushrooms are identified by the presence of gills. The best-known family of Agaricales is Agaricaceae, having mushroom fruiting bodies. Some mushrooms are poisonous, for example, Death cap (*Amanita phalloides*), *Conocybe filaris*, Webcaps (*Cortinarius* species), etc. The poisonous mushrooms can be identified by the color of their gills. They mostly have white gills or ringed stems and also have an underground structure called volva. So to identify it, you may need to dig it out from the ground.

Another type of mushrooms is Hallucinogenic mushrooms. These mushrooms are also known as “Magic mushrooms” and “Psilocybin Mushrooms.” This type of mushrooms contains hallucinogenic properties; therefore, they have been used in medicines too.

History and Background of Psilocybin Mushrooms

As mentioned in history, some mushrooms have been used for religious purposes and in different rituals. These mushrooms, which have been of great importance according to a religious point of view, are mostly Psilocybin mushrooms. These mind-catching bodies have been an important part of cultures deprived of time and space. Many religions and philosophies of the world have been influenced by these "Magic Mushrooms."

Reko, Richard E. Schultes, Roger Heim, and R. Gordon Wasson are the lucky scientists and researchers who are responsible to re-discover the remains of ancient usage of Psilocybin mushrooms. They discovered that the old native Mesoamerican people used Psilocybin mushrooms in their rituals and ceremonies. Their research showed that modern-day mushroom cultures have ancestral links with the Psilocybin mushrooms, which were used in the religious practices of some civilizations like Aztec and Mayan. History shows that the Aztec people had so much belief in a specific Psilocybin mushroom (Psilocybe Mexicana) that they named it Teonanacatl, which means "God's Flesh." A Franciscan in the 16th century went on an expedition with a team and reported about the beliefs of Aztec about "God's Flesh," but misguided Catholics. Catholics were running a campaign against Paganism at that time, and they were misguided about the usage of mushrooms. They restricted the use of Psilocybin mushrooms as they thought that pagans worshipped these mushrooms. This all resulted in the planned demise of this culture, but they couldn't destroy some evidence.

The research and reports by Franciscan Bernardino De Sahagun are the ultimate sources of knowledge about usage of this type of mushrooms by Aztec tribes.

Further Improvement in the Discovery of Psilocybin Mushrooms

This situation gave rise to a new belief, with a mix of Christianity and mushroom rituals. R. Gordon Wasson and his team also discovered an indigenous healer named Maria Sabina, who practiced the use of Psilocybin mushrooms to heal many mental, physical, and spiritual problems. People said that she had specific "Magic Mushrooms." In search of these, the people of America came to know about the Psilocybin mushrooms of Mexico. When more people came to know about Maria Sabina, her popularity reached outside of America, and many people searched for her due to her magical mushrooms.

Not only in Mexico and America, but the traditional and religious use of Psilocybin mushrooms had also been found in ancient European culture. The philosophers Aristotle, Plato, Homer, and Sophocles were seen in history participating in the ceremonies in a different temple Demeter, in front of the goddess of agriculture. Strange types of ceremonies used to be held in those temples where people believed that they got changed after spending a night there. A conference about mushrooms was held in 1977 in Europe in which different psychoactive mushrooms of the world were discussed, and researchers got a new thing to research on.

Wasson and his team were the first Ethnomycologists, while Jonathan and his team proved themselves to be the second generation of Ethnomycologists. Human history has dramatic effects of Psilocybin mushrooms and many more yet to come. If we talk about the history of natural cultivation of Psilocybin mushrooms, a French mycologist Roger Heim was the pioneer who cultivated many Psilocybin species successfully, in the 1950s. He used the materials which were brought by Wasson and his team from their journey. Then the work started, and many Psilocybin mushroom species were discovered until the end of the1970s, and still there are many mushrooms yet to be discovered.

Classification of Psilocybin Mushrooms

Psilocybin mushrooms are types of mushrooms that contain two active compounds psilocybin and psilocin, having hallucinogenic properties. They belong to different genera like *Copelandia, Gymnopilus, Inocybe, Mycena, Panaeolus, Pholiotina, Pluteus,* and *Psilocybe.*

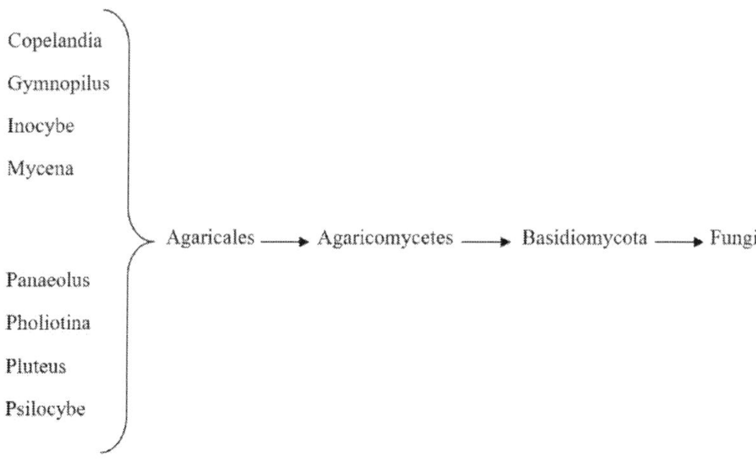

All these genera of order Agaricales contain hallucinogenic properties. Table 1.2 shows the number of species and examples of each genus.

Genera	Species	Example
Copelandia	Few	*Panaeolus cambodginiensis*
Gymnopilus	200	*Gymnopilus cyanopalmicola*
Inocybe	1400	*Inocybe aeruginascens*
Mycena	500 above	*Mycena cyanorrhiza*
Panaeolus	98	*Panaeolus cyanescens*
Pholiotina	100 above	*Pholiota gummosa*
Pluteus	300	*Pluteus brunneidiscus*
Psilocybe	500 above	*Psilocybe cubensis*

Table: 1.3: Genera of class Agaricales and its hallucinogenic species

Reproduction and Lifecycle of Mushrooms

Most of the fungi species have a sexual reproduction process. Sexual reproduction occurs when a new organism forms by the recombination of male and female genetic material. In scientific language, this genetic material is in the form of gametes. The genetic material or gametes of fungi are spores. The structure of a spore is well defined after the invention of the microscope. Otherwise, spores cannot be seen with the naked eye. According to microscopic observations, the spore is a cell protected by an outer wall, in a compact shape, and it is able to keep itself dormant for years. It makes itself active only when it finds a suitable environment for it. Most of the fungal species grow in a moist and humid environment, so when spore finds such an environment, they start the reproduction process. Take the example of Basidiomycetes whose spores are present on their basidia, which have a structure like baseball-bat, and they are present in the lining of gills (of mushrooms). These basidia are in a beautiful pattern arranged on the underside of the mushroom cap. This cap or pileus is attached to a stem of cylindrical shape, and mycologists call it "stipe."

Spore Detachment

Spores are of purple color when observed under a microscope. The outer end of basidium, which is horn-shaped and protrude outside, is called sterigma. It is an interesting fact that air under the cap of mushrooms, around the gills, is cooler as compared to the air on the upper side. It is because of the evaporation mechanism where the upper side faces sun rays, and the moist air on the underside becomes cool. During the evaporation process, the water around spores becomes condense when the air gets cool, this process creates a droplet at the place where the spore joins with its stem. Droplet gets growing until it loses its tension and can't grow anymore. As a result, the water in the droplet spreads over the spore's body, which forces the spore to move towards sterigma. When it touches sterigma, it faces an elastic reaction, thus returning with force: we can say it faces a catapulted action by sterigma. As a result, spore tends to fall, and the wind takes it away from its source with many of other spores.

The Spore Dispersal

The wind or air takes the spores away and throws them in fields, walls or anywhere else. When these spores find a suitable environment, they grow; otherwise, they remain dormant for years. Spores spread by wind are also displaced by animals and birds. For example, wind threw the psilocybin mushroom spore in a field, a goat came and ate the spores with grass, but it can't digest those spores as they have good armor. When the goat passes feces, those spores come out as such, and if they find a suitable environment there, they grow into a new psilocybin mushroom.

Fungi, when growing, contain a large number of hyphae. Hyphae are defined as the long filamentous cells, tubular-shaped, which get divided at the upper tips, creating a fork-like structure. A network of hyphae is called "Mycelium." Mycelium appears as white, hair-like growths on food or soil surface (called a substrate). Most of the fungi remain undifferentiated in the form of mycelium; only some of them grow into structures like mushrooms, puffballs, bracket fungi, etc. You may observe that the surface which is affected by fungus start to degrade. Actually, there are digestive enzymes secreted by mycelium, which degrade the substrate into organic molecules, and then mycelium absorbs those molecules as food.

The life Cycle of Psilocybin Mushrooms

Spores, when converting into mycelium colonies, eat the substrate and produce more spores. Those spores tend to look for spores from other colonies, for mating. It is because fungi want to spread diversity, and for this purpose, it forms different mating types. Whenever spores of one gender find suitable spores of another gender, they start mating. The cells of mycelium are monokaryotic and have a haploid nucleus (half genetic material). This slow, fuzzy material, when fusing with another half genetic material (haploid nucleus), it forms a cell containing two nuclei, this forming dikaryotic cell. This process is mostly specific to Basidiomycetes, where the nuclei remain separated even in a single cell. This phenomenon is different from other organisms because, in this process, two nuclei remain in a single cell until they combine inside the basidium. In short, the fungus intercourse starts very early and ends very late. The process keeps on going until this mycelium transforms into a fruiting body like mushrooms. Following is a simple illustration of a mushroom life cycle, which represents the life cycle of almost all genera, but actually, this illustration is of the life cycle of Psilocybin mushroom.

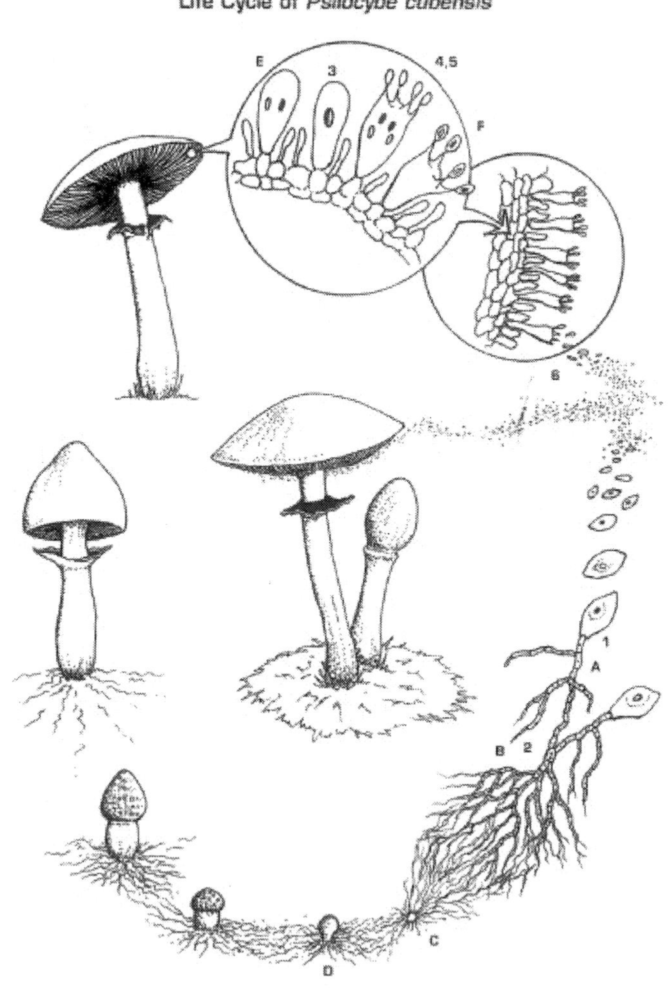

Life Cycle of *Psilocybe cubensis*

Figure: Life Cycle of Psilocybe cubensis

Short Summary

Mushrooms are not new in the human diet; they were used by indigenous people a long time ago. Humans used to eat mushrooms even at the time when they didn't know their names. They were not only part of dishes but also the part of religious and cultural rituals. However, mushrooms are not only edibles, but they are also death caps as well as hallucinogens. There are thousands of mushrooms in the world that belong to the kingdom fungi. Some of the species of fungi are too diverse that they don't match a single morphological feature with each other. Mushrooms are actually fruiting bodies of fungi, which are diverse in shape and nature. Edible mushrooms are even different in taste, some are normal, and some are very delicious. Hallucinogenic mushrooms belong to the order Agaricales of basidiomycetes. Almost all classes of order Agaricales are Psilocybin mushrooms, containing hallucinogenic properties. Psilocybin mushrooms are those which contain two specific psychoactive compounds that are also used in some drugs. This book is about Psilocybin mushrooms; therefore, the evolution, occurrences, and other properties of these mushrooms will be discussed in later chapters.

Chapter Two

Occurrence of Psilocybin Mushrooms

Psilocybin mushrooms contain two compounds: psilocybin and psilocin. So, Psilocybin mushrooms are hallucinogenic mushrooms due to the presence of these two compounds. If we look at other mushrooms and their evolution, these compounds are not present in all mushrooms. It means that when these mushrooms evolved, they didn't have such hallucinogenic properties. If we look at the evolution of mushrooms, they were not like they are now. They evolved from Pseudomonas and then puffballs evolved and then morels, and now the latest umbrella shaped mushrooms. In the same way, different mushrooms adapted different properties from environment. Psilocybin mushrooms, which are also called Psychedelic mushrooms or magic mushrooms due to their magical affects on human mind, have these psychoactive compounds, specifically. A study was conducted by a researcher, Jason Slot, at The Ohio State University. He claimed that these

Psilocybin mushrooms have wide biological lineage, and different morphological appearance.

Environment has stressors as well as opportunities, and these two factors are also responsible for physical and genetic changes in organisms. Horizontal gene transfer is a phenomena which occurs in nature to develop changes at genetic level by transferring genetic material from other organisms. Slot believed that Psilocybin mushrooms are those which got hallucinogenic genes from such gene transfers. The examination of psychedelic mushrooms paralleled with the examination of other fungi (which are not hallucinogenic) showed some differences in genetic material. All hallucinogenic mushrooms (Psilocybin mushrooms) share a cluster of five genes which were not present in other fungi.

How and Why Psilocybin Mushrooms Got Those Different Genes

Psilocybin mushrooms have characteristics to create hallucinations in humans as well as they have ability to send human mind into an altered state. This is due to the presence of Psilocybin, which is present due to that cluster of Psilocybin producing genes. Study showed that those genes may have been transferred from some fungus-eating insects. As these mushrooms grow in an environment with insects, animal manure, rotten woods and other things like these, insects used to eat fungus, and as a result, protection was developed in those mushrooms by production of Psilocybin. It not only alters human mind but it also affects insect's brain. It suppresses a neurotransmitter in insects which lowers the appetite so they don't tend to eat these mushrooms. Eating Psilocybin mushrooms doesn't kill insects but it alters their brain and working capabilities. History shows that Psilocybin mushrooms have also been used as insect repellents even when the human didn't know about their exact uses. Many Psilocybin mushrooms don't share much genetic material except this cluster of five genes which shows that they come from different biological backgrounds. Sharing of this psilocybin producing cluster of genes shows that this horizontal gene transfer occurred for protective and evolutionary purpose, for the survival of these mushrooms. So, decoding of these genes can open new doors of research, to study these genes and find their impacts on human mind and body.

Habitats of Psilocybin Mushrooms

Psilocybin mushrooms grow all over the world but mostly they are found in fields and forests. They are saprophytes like other fungi, so they cannot make their food like plants. Instead, they usually grow on dead plant material and were restricted to narrow areas before humans found them. Some ecological and natural destructions like land sliding, floods, volcanoes and hurricanes created suitable habitats for Psilocybin mushrooms, by leaving the environmental effects. These natural processes are also responsible for traveling of Psilocybin mushrooms from one place to other. When humans started cutting trees, these mushrooms found their place on wooden chips and rotted woods etc. They adapted themselves to the human environment so much, that they started growing in gardens, near houses, in fields etc. It shows the relation of Psilocybin mushrooms with human activities. Human activities and climate changes turned many green areas into deserts, but the growth of Psilocybin mushrooms continued, and they continued to adapt themselves according to environment.

Depending upon the evidences, Psilocybin mushrooms have five major habitats, including:

- Grasslands
- Dung deposits
- Burned lands
- Riparian zones (flooded areas)
- Moss lands

Grasslands

Grassland habitats, which are mostly wet and swampy lands, support the growth of Psilocybin mushrooms. These moist environments are very supportive habitats for fungi, therefore some Psilocybin mushrooms are specific to grasslands. In such habitats, mostly conic shaped, tall, thin and small Psilocybes grow, for example *P.strictipes, P.liniformans, P.semilanceata, P.mexicana, and P.samuiensis.* Most of them grow on matted grass bases, camel grass or on lemon grass. Some tryptamine producing grasses are also a good habitat for Psilocybes, because these grasses have a potential impact on the production of psilocybin and psilocin. Canary grasses have dimethytrypton content and they are also good habitats for psilocybin. It means that grasses have different impacts on growth and properties of Psilocybin mushrooms. Their environment has some morphological impacts which help to identify grassland psilocybin mushrooms easily. Some Psilocybin mushrooms from grasslands are from Sclerotia culture as they are hard in shape and have nut-like structures. Therefore some grassland psilocybin mushrooms are known to produce sclerotia which can survive environmental disasters, for example *P.mexicana*, *Conocybe cyanapus* etc. Most of the grasslands' species of Psilocybin mushrooms like moist and humid environments, and they are humus loving. These species grow in red clays or dark loams and are usually attached to tall grass so they are easy to pick. The grassland species of Psilocybin mushrooms are distributed and spread by different grazing animals like sheep, horses, cattle, yaks, water buffalo etc. Usually, these mushrooms remain undigested in an animal's body, and excreted through their feces, thus leaving these mushrooms to grow in dung places.

Dung Deposits

The species growing at grasslands and dung deposits share geographical niche. Most of the species which grow in grasslands also grow in dung deposits. As mentioned earlier, the animals who graze on grass excrete undigested spores of mushrooms in their feces and are responsible for the growth of Psilocybin mushrooms in dung deposits. Dung deposits are not permanent habitats: they are short lived habitats. So, the Psilocybin mushrooms grow there but cannot last for long time. *Psilocybe cubensis* is a dung dwelling species and its co-occurrence with a grassland species *Psilocybe mexicana,* is an example of relation of grasslands and dung deposit habitats. Other well-known species habiting dung deposits include *Psilocybe coprophila, Panaeolus cyanescens* and *Panaeolus subbalteatus,* etc. The dung of Cascade Mountains of Pacific Northwest are large habitats of Psilocybin mushrooms and provide a easy to find habitat for these mushrooms.

Burned Lands

Although burned lands are not very good for the growth of Psilocybin mushrooms, sometimes good fruiting can be found there. In some regions like Central Oregon, there is a practice to burn fields and grass-seed lands, then their re-growth. Such lands have the evidences of growth of fruiting of Psilocybin mushrooms, like *Psilocybe strictipes.* The natural rebirth of these lands supports the growth and development of Psilocybin mushrooms. The soil erosion, cracking, etc. can occur in burned lands. But, the growth of Psilocybin mushrooms can also be supported by flooding etc.

Riparian Zones and Disturbed Habitats

Riparian zone is the area which is a link or connection between land area and stream or river. They are mostly created by flooding in rivers. When flow in rivers is at its peak, it passes over the plants and tress, thus causing some damage but after that overflow, a riparian zone forms. These regions have high sand content but are a great source of biomass. Many species of Psilocybin mushrooms grow in these riparian zones because they find suitable environment there. For example, *Psilocybin quebecens* is a popular species which grows in riparian zones. The mushroom species which grow there also grow in disturbed regions. Disturbed habitats are those which are formed by natural disasters like floods, earthquakes, etc. Hot springs and Geysers are also a combination of riparian zones and disturbed habitats caused by different changes in nature. For examples, *Psilocybe Cyanofiberillosa* is a psilocybin species living in such habitats. Lets discuss disturbed habitats in detail.

Gardens

Gardens come under the category of disturbed habitats because of the continuous tilling process. They are excellent habitats for Psilocybin mushrooms. Gardens help these mushrooms by daily watering, soil amendments, and growth of plants. Examples of species growing in gardens include, *Psilocybe baeocystis, Psilocybe caerulescens, Psilocybe Stuntzii* etc.

Woodlands

Woodlands are mostly populated with coniferous trees and other subtropical plants. It is a very suitable habitat for the growth of Psilocybin mushrooms. The humid and moist environment and soil promote the growth of these mushrooms and many other species.

Moss Lands

Moss lands are another habitat of Psilocybin mushrooms as they are covered with Sphagnum. Sphagnum is a popular peat moss which can be a substrate for Psilocybin mushrooms. Moss lands are not very good habitats for these mushrooms.

Psilocybin Mushrooms in Different Regions of the World

Psilocybin mushrooms are not restricted to one region of the world. The use of Psilocybin mushrooms by churches also have some evidences. For example, reports were received from Mexico, Southern Nigeria, Brazil and Russia that Christian churches have the practice of using a mysterious type of mushrooms (dried) with unknown identifications. With the shift of climate, new ecosystems were formed and the transformation continued. Jungles became savannas and savannas became deserts. Some deserts became jungles or savannas etc. Depending upon the supporting climate and habitats, Psilocybin mushrooms are distributed in different regions of the world.

Northern Algeria

Important Psilocybin species have been found in the region of Northern Algeria. One important specie found there is "*Psilocybe cyanescens.*" These types of mushrooms also comes under the category of riparian habitat. In the sandy soils and wood debris of Northern Algeria, a rare species of Psilocybin mushrooms, *P.mairei,* is found. Reports have been received from Northern Africa about the presence of these mushrooms on the surface.

Northern Africa

In 1995, a researcher from Italy, Giorgio Samorini, found evidences that Psilocybin mushrooms were used in churches of Southern Nigeria.

Pacific Northwest

In the Pacific Northwest, about four thousand species of mushrooms are present, according to authentic reports. Out of these four thousand species, more than a dozen are Psilocybin mushrooms. Mexico is rich in these mushrooms.

In Europe

The characteristics of *Psilocybe semilanceata* were not clear before. A research team including A. Hofmann and R. Heim studied the samples of this species deeply and got services of a mycologist C. Furrer who studied the fruiting. These samples were collected from Switzerland and France. The study revealed in 1963 that this specie contains Psilocybin even in dried samples of mushrooms. This was the first time when Psilocybin mushroom species were discovered in Europe.

Germany

In the 1960s, Psilocybin mushrooms were also found in Germany. Recently, a team of researchers and mycologists, Jochen Gartz and Georg Wiedemann by Funghi Enterprise Germany, found the bluish Psilocybin mushrooms in Germany and named them *Psilocybe germanica.* This specie was found in the soils having wood and debris. Researchers reported that this specie may have wide distribution.

Scotland and England

A popular specie of Psilocybin mushrooms, *Psilocybe semilanceata,* which is also known as liberty cap and magic mushroom is found in Scotland and England. Its samples were collected and verified. In England, the growths of these mushrooms have been seen in Shropshire and Staffordshire in fungi season. Another specie of Psilocybe mushrooms, *Psilocybe cyanescens,* is found in England, near mulched plant beds in lignin-rich substrates and in the areas rich in wood chips. Other species growing in UK include *P.Fimetaria, Gymnopilus purpuratus, Panaeolus olivaceous* etc.

Austria

Austria is a region of Europe with suitable climate for flora. Large areas of Austria are covered with woods, so it creates a suitable habitat for Psilocybe mushrooms. The species found in Austria include: *Panaeolus cyanescens, Gymnopillus sp., Inocybe coelestium, Inocybe corydalina, Inocybe haemacta, Inocybe tricolor, Panaeolus cinctulus, Panaeolus fimicola, Psilocybe cyanescens, Psilocybe semilanceata,* and *Psilocybe serbic.*

Belgium, Bulgaria, Czech Republic, Denmark

The caves of Belgium, rich in limestone, are best for the growth of many Psilocybin mushrooms. There are evidences of the presence of Psilocybin species in Bulgaria as well as in Czech Republic: they grow on wood chips and rotting bars. In the mosslands of Denmark, some popular species are found with hallucinogenic properties. Important species of Psilocybin mushrooms growing in these countries include *Gymnopilus sp, Inocybe haemacta, Psilocybe cyanescens, Psilocybe fimetaria, Psilocybe semilanceata,* etc.

Other European countries with a variety of Psilocybin mushroom species include France, Faroes Islands, Estonia, Finland, Greece, Lithuania, Norway, Serbia, etc.

North America

The third largest continent is North America, which is known for its beautiful islands and changing seasons. The weather varies from dry to steamy tropics. This region is mostly warm in summer and cold in winter overall, but in some areas, there are harsh winters and short summers. These changing climates support the growth of Psilocybin mushrooms.

United States of America

Some geographical regions of USA are suitable for the growth of Psilocybin mushrooms. But in southern states, only liberty caps are found in those regions. Some popular species of Psilocybin mushrooms which are found in USA, according to some evidences, are, *Conocybe cyanopus, Gymnopilus junonius, Gymnopilus aeruginosus, Psilocybe cubensis, Panaeolus fimicola, Psilocybe cyanescens, Psilocybe baeocystis, Psilocybe tampanens, Psilocybe mammilata, Gymnopilus luteofolius,* etc.

Canada

The climate and soil in Canada are different in regions of Canada. Two fifth of the Canadian forests have supportive environment for the growth of Psilocybin mushrooms, therefore a wide variety can be found there. Some of the species of Psilocybin mushrooms found in Canada include, *Panaeolus cinctulus, Psilocybe baeocystis, Psilocybe cyanofibrillosa, Psilocybe cyanescens, Psilocybe cubensis, Psilocybe fimetaria, Psilocybe sierra, Psilocybe sylvatica, Psilocybe strictipes, Psilocybe stuntzii, Psilocybe subfimetaria,* etc.

Mexico

The history of evidences of Psilocybin mushrooms and their uses in Mexico have been discussed earlier in Chapter 1. The flora of Mexico is varied due to its climate. The hardwoods, jungles and caves of Mexico are very well known for the growth of Psilocybin mushrooms. Thousands of species of Psilocybin mushrooms grow there, some of which include:

- *Paneolus fimicola*
- *Panaeolus cyanescens*
- *Panaeolus venezolanus*
- *Panaeolus tropicalis*
- *Conocybe banderillensis*
- *Psilocybe rzedowskii*
- *Psilocybe singer*
- *Psilocybe uxpanapensis*
- *Psilocybe veraecrucis*
- *Psilocybe weldenii*
- *Psilocybe caerulescens*
- *Psilocybe fagicola*
- *Psilocybe herrerae*
- *Psilocybe mammillata*
- *Psilocybe schultesii*
- *Psilocybe wassonoirum*
- *Psilocybe xalapensis*
- *Psilocybe yungensis*
- *Psilocybe armandii*
- *Psilocybe mexicana*
- *Psilocybe pseudobullacae*

- *Psilocybe cubensis*
- *Psilocybe subcubensis*
- *Psilocybe muliercula*
- *Psilocybe zapotecorum*
- *Psilocybe tuxtlensis*
- *Psillocybe chaconii*
- *Psilocybe subtropicalis*
- *Psilocybe neoxalapensis*
- *Psilocybe isabelae*
- *Psilocybe naematoliformis*

South America

A large area of South America is known to have tropical climate. Some areas are too dry like Atacama Desert and some are rainy like Amazon Basin. The temperature in the mountains of South America is mostly 15 degrees while the temperature in the tropics is mostly 38 degrees. The variations in the climate support the growth of Psilocybin mushrooms, therefore many of its species are native to some regions of South America. The countries of South America where the species of Psilocybin mushrooms are found include, Argentina, Bahamas, Bermuda, Belize, Bolivia, Brazil, Colombia, Costa Rica, Ecuador, El Salvador, Guatemala, Panama, Peru, Uruguay and Venezuela. The species of Psilocybin mushrooms, found in these regions, include, *Panaeolus cinctulus, Panaeolus fimicolaPsilocybe wrightii, Psilocybe zapotecorum, Gymnopilus sp., Psilocybe cordispora, Psilocybe cubensis, Psilocybe blattariopsis, Psilocybe banderillensis, Psilocybe strictipes, Psilocybe subfimetaria, Psilocybe angustipleurocystidiata, Psilocybe antioquiensis,* etc.

Asia

The southeast regions of Asia have wet climate while inside is mostly dry. Across the southern and eastern sections, the monsoon circulation brings rainfall in specific seasons. The rainy season creates a suitable environment for the growth of Psilocybin mushrooms. Some popular species found in Asia are *Gymnopilus sp., Panaeolus cinctulus, Panaeolus cambodginiensis, Panaeolus cyanescens,* and *Psilocybe cyanescens,* etc. The manure of cattle and buffaloes is a source of displacement of spores of these mushrooms. The Asian countries which have authentic evidences of Psilocybin mushroom growth, are, Cambodia, China, India, Indonesia, Japan, Sri Lanka, Thailand and Vietnam. The common species which are found in these countries are, *Psilocybe samulensis, Psilocybe thailandensis, Panaeolus cyanescens, Panaeolus rubricaulis, Gymnopilus aeruginosus, Gymnoilus junonius, Panaeolus cyanescens, Psilocybe indica, Psilocybe natarajanji, Psilocybe wayanadensis,* etc.

Cultivation of Psilocybin Mushrooms

We have discussed the natural occurrences of mushrooms, where they grow naturally when they find the suitable environment. But, due to hallucinogenic properties of these Psilocybin mushrooms, researchers and experts cultivate and grow these mushrooms on large scales. Cultivation of mushrooms requires understanding for growth conditions and nutrient requirements. In nutrient requirements and cultivation conditions, Psilocybin mushrooms are not much different from other edible types. The natural propagation of Psilocybin mushrooms has been discussed earlier, the involvement of wind to disperse the spores and the growth of mycelium when conditions are favorable. The mushroom growers and collectors know that, naturally, there are long dry periods for mushrooms, when no growth is seen in many regions, and there are times of maximum mushroom yields in a part of a year.

The Growth Conditions

Psilocybe mushrooms are saprophytic like the other fungi. They start fruiting after the complete growth of their mycelia and when they find the following environmental conditions:

- 95 to 100% humidity
- Low temperature
- Reduction in the concentration of carbon dioxide
- Light exposure

In many regions, these conditions are present naturally but when it is absent, the mushroom growers recreate these conditions in glass containers. Before cultivation on large scales, Psilocybe mushrooms are grown on agar for trial and then go for large scale cultivation. It is common in all species of mushrooms that their fruiting starts during the fall season. When leaves and woods fall on to the ground, the mycelia take the opportunity and start the growth on these substrates.

The large-scale cultivation other than natural growth of Psilocybin mushrooms is called artificial cultivation. The mushrooms growers tend to create the natural conditions for growth. These attempts also lead to finding new substrates for the growth of these mushrooms. The artificial cultivation methods need clear environment, free from bacteria and other microorganisms. Laminar flow cabinets are used to keep the cultures of Psilocybin mushrooms free from foreign particles. Inside these containers, they create sterile environment. Different methods are used for large scale cultivation.

First Method for Cultivation

One method of Psilocybin mushroom cultivation is by collecting the spores of these mushrooms. The spores, from the gills, are collected by a microscopic method and they are stored in sterilized water. This solution is then poured onto the 1.5% agar medium contained malt extract, with various concentrations of required nutrients. Let the spores from different species germinate into mycelia. Before growth, all the cultures (containing spores) are placed in an autoclave to remove any other substances or microorganisms.

They start germination and this results in the formation of mycelia. These monokaryotic mycelia then combine and form diakaryotic mycelia, thus producing different strains of

Psilocybin mushrooms. Cross breeding experiments on these growths lead to differentiating between different species of mushrooms. For example, the mycelia of *Psilocybe bihemica* and *Psilocybe cyanesens* don't fuse together. After growth, these mycelia can be transferred to fields for the large-scale cultivation.

Second Method for Cultivation

A second common method of psilocybin mushroom cultivation is, using the cuttings from naturally growing mushrooms. In this method, a small tissue is taken from the unopened mushroom fruiting body with a sterilized knife by creating a sterilized environment. This tissue is then placed on nutrient agar where the mycelia grow due to the presence of required conditions and nutrients. The benefits of using this tissue cutting method is that the new psilocybe mushroom, grown from these cultures, is genetically identical with source mushrooms. So, the researchers can have exactly the same variety of mushrooms on large scale. Some strains of wild mushrooms take a long time to grow, but researchers continue experimentations.

First, this cultivation method was introduced by R. Heim in 1956 when he and his team used this method for the cultivation of popular Psilocybe species *Psilocybe mexicana.* He took those strains from Mexico and germinated them in Paris. He was successful in growing these strains of Psilocybin mushrooms on compost media. Compost media is then used for the growth of many psilocybe strains as it is a nutrient rich substrate. The material provided by this scientist was also used by Hofmann and his team to isolate the psilocybin and psilocin compounds first time. Heim and Caileux have major role in introducing the artificial cultivation method for various strains of Psilocybe mushrooms. Their discovery became the base for the large-scale harvest of several alkaloids. *Psilocybe cyanescens,* which is an American species, when grown on malt agar medium, turned blue, while, when same strain was grown on liquid medium, no blue color was observed. The reason behind this process is still hidden. While growing *Panaeolussubbalteatus* , H.J Brodie observed bluish-green formations, when he cultivated this strain on malt agar. This is not a specie which usually turns blue, therefore Brodie said that his cultures were contaminated with molds.

The large-scale cultivation of Psilocybin mushrooms began in the 1950s and above-mentioned scientists were pioneers who introduced such cultivation methods. The process of cultivation continued and many strains of different species of Psilocybes were grown on large scale by using laboratory grown cultures (tissues of spores taken from wild species).

Home Cultivation

The cultivation kits for Psilocybin mushrooms have been available for 20 years and are easily accessible by mushroom growers. Therefore, mushrooms can also be cultivated at home. Mostly, home growers are only successful in growing mycelia, because producing fruiting bodies in vitro is hard. Only the cultivation of *Psilocybe cebensis* with its fruiting bodies is easy: it is an exception.

Cultivation of Psilocybin mushrooms at homes, and home cultures require extra care and attention. Some Magic mushrooms are native to some areas, so home growers may not find any difficulty in growing them.

Some Other Methods of Cultivation

Some other methods of cultivation of Psilocybin mushrooms include:

- Agar spore germination (similar to the one discussed before)
- Cardboard Disc Spore Germination
- Agar to agar transfers

The Status of Cultivation

These cultivation methods are not only used to grow these Psilocybin mushrooms but the cultures are also used to isolate specific compounds like Psilocybin and Psilocin and some other required chemicals. Cultivation in laboratories is used for research purpose. Scientists and researchers have been doing work on these mushrooms for years, because of amazing characteristics. In some countries, the large scale field cultivation of Psilocybin mushrooms is not legal due to its hallucinogenic nature. They might be used in crimes, so some countries have prohibited the cultivation of these mushrooms. The countries where large scale cultivation of Psilocybin mushrooms is illegal are Australia, Belgium, Bolivia, Canada, Indonesia, Japan, etc.

Short Summary

This chapter covered the history and evolution of Psilocybin mushrooms and their existences in different regions of the world. These mushrooms evolved from simple fungus and developed fruiting bodies, which have been used for different purposes, for years. Mexico is the largest home for Psilocybin mushrooms but they are also found in many countries of Asia, Europe, North America, etc. The discovery of amazing properties of these mushrooms lead to the formation of different cultivation methods for it.

CHAPTER THREE

The Biology of Psilocybin Mushrooms

The outer look of Psilocybin mushrooms is the straight stem, open flat cap, wide and dark, brown in color. Inexperienced persons cannot properly identify the Psilocybin mushrooms, and they may mix them with other mushrooms. Many mushrooms are toxic and may lead to death; therefore, a layperson must not search psilocybin mushrooms without the help of an expert. Experts can easily identify these mushrooms based on their experience. The Psilocybin mushrooms are mostly identified by their gills, which are white in color. These gills have linings in which spores are present. These spores are responsible for the spread of these mushrooms through different dispersal procedures. Not all gilled mushrooms are Psilocybin mushrooms. Psilocybin mushrooms have brown or black spores inside the gills, and sometimes these mushrooms have bluish bruises.

It has been discussed earlier that Psilocybin mushrooms are saprophyte, like all other fungi. They have the same internal structure like other fungi with a cap attached to a stem having gills inside. The stem is attached to the volva, and volva stands on hyphae, the hair-like structures protruding out, and attaches this mushroom to the ground - these are called mycelium. Almost all fungi have this structure with little exceptions, mentioned before.

The Life Cycle of Magic Mushrooms

The hyphae of mycelia of magic mushrooms pass through plasmogamy which is a process where the cytoplasm from two different parent cells fuses, but leaves the nuclei infused. Means, cytoplasm combines, but nuclei remain haploid. Psilocybin mushrooms have haploid gametes, i.e. (n) instead of (2n). They form a diploid mycelium from a haploid parent. When the environment is suitable, this mycelium grows into mushrooms. When the karyogamy occurs in the cells, they result in the formation of gills. Karyogamy is a process in which the two unfused haploid nuclei fuse to form diploid nuclei. To understand the life cycle of Psilocybin mushrooms, keep these points in mind:

- Spores release and disperse through wind
- Find a suitable environment and germinate
- Mating
- Plasmogamy occurs
- Dikaryotic mycelium
- Gills form containing basidia

- Haploid nuclei
- Karyogamy occurs
- Diploid nuclei form
- Meiosis occurs (formation of basidiospores)
- Release of spores
- Cycle continues

With slight differences, all mushrooms go through this life cycle. The internal structure and chemistry of all mushrooms are the same with some differences. For example, Psilocybin mushrooms contain Psilocybe, and it is present in these mushrooms due to horizontal gene transfer. The biological and chemical properties of these mushrooms will be discussed further.

Identification of Psilocybin Mushrooms

Many people mix these with other mushrooms. To identify Psilocybin mushrooms, high expertise and experience are required as wrong identifications can lead to health dangers. Some people may confuse magic mushrooms with others, and when they eat them, they may face mental health issues because they don't know the proper way to use these hallucinogenic mushrooms. Some mushrooms are deadly poisonous and the collectors may collect wrong mushrooms instead of Psilocybin mushrooms. So, a mushroom collector must have keen observation and knowledge about psilocybin mushrooms.

Hofmann and his team were the first who identified the Psilocybin mushrooms successfully using the laboratory methods. The real identifications were made in 1958; before that, people used to identify these mushrooms only through their outer look and assumptions. Hofmann and his team members changed the game. They used *Psilocybe mexicana* to grow its cultures in the laboratory and then grow its fruiting bodies, sclerotia, and mycelium using these cultures. They also observed that the same psychoactive activity was present in both dried and fresh samples of *Psilocybe mexicana.* That was the time when the compounds behind the psychoactive activity and hallucinogenic properties of these mushrooms were discovered. Improper identification of mushrooms may lead to death, so one must understand the shape and structure of psilocybe mushrooms to avoid misidentifications. As these mushrooms have hallucinogenic properties, they can alter the human mind, thus producing psychological effects. These effects can be for a short time period or longer, depending upon the quantity of mushroom taken and the power of that specific type.

To identify magic mushrooms, one must consider these points:

- Brown colored mushrooms (Brown fruiting bodies)
- Having white gills underside
- Most of the psilocybe mushrooms have a ring around their neck, so consider that too
- Spore color (mostly purple-colored spores are of psilocybe mushrooms)

This is not the ultimate guide for mushroom identification, so if you find such mushrooms and you need to identify if they are magic mushrooms or not, check them in your laboratory to confirm. You can also use spore printing as an easy method to discover those mushrooms. Use a piece of paper, and put spores on them, then check the color that they leave on tissue paper. It can help to identify the psilocybin mushrooms. Thus, two important methods of mushroom identification are:

- Spore printing
- Bluing reaction

Spore Printing

The spore color is the most important thing in mushroom identification. If you are a mushroom collector, or you are in search of Psilocybe mushrooms for some purpose, consider their spores. Take the mushrooms and put them in polythene bags, but remember, don't tighten the bags because they have to breathe. If mushrooms become dry, the spores will change their color, which will not help in identification. So, use fresh and live mushrooms.

Open the polythene bag, take a mushroom and cut it. There is a proper way to cut those mushrooms. Choose flattened mushrooms to cut and separate their caps from the stem using a knife. Put the gills of the mushrooms (underside of the cap) on the paper or tissue paper and cover it with some glass to increase the level of hydration and decrease the chance of dehydration. Keeping the air currents away will give good spore print. If the gills are humid or wet, they will give a good spore print. If they leave purple or dark purple color on tissue paper, they are surely psilocybin mushrooms. This process is called spore printing because the spore leaves its print on the tissue paper for identification purpose. According to the symmetry of the gills, the spores will print on the paper, showing the mass and color of spores. After identification, you can label the print, and you can use these spore prints for mushroom cultivation in the future.

Bluing Reaction

The second important strategy to identify psilocybin mushrooms is their bluing reaction. Many psilocybin mushrooms have common properties that become the source of their identification. Most of the psilocybin mushrooms become bluish or bluish-green when they are bruised. Mushrooms do not only get bruises when they are crushed: bluish bruises can show when they are simply handled or picked. This bluing reaction shows that there is something different in these mushrooms. Scientists and researchers are in search of finding the reason behind this bluing reaction. One reason behind this bluing is the degradation of psilocybe and psilocin compounds. Some other unknown compounds also participate in this reaction. This is the most important identity of Psilocybin mushrooms as this property is not shown by other types. But, on the other hand, some psilocybe species don't show this blue color and no bluish bruises.

After some time, researchers also found that there are some poisonous mushrooms with bluish bruises, but they have no psilocybe. For example, the *Hygrphorus conicus* is a poisonous mushroom species that shows a bluish reaction when picking it up. So, now the bluish reaction is a primary parameter for Psilocybin mushroom identification, but not the least parameter. A trained person is needed to identify the correct species.Experts can also check the psilocybin mushrooms in labs to confirm the presence of specific psilocin and psilocybe compounds.

The Narrowing Down Technique for Identification

If someone wants to get expertise in the identification and collection of psilocybin mushrooms, he must follow the narrowing down technique. First, collect the mushrooms which you doubt are psilocybin mushrooms. Collect conical-shaped cap mushrooms, with a long stem, dark brown pointed caps, and brown gills. Place these mushrooms in plastic bags. Bring them to the laboratory and let them dry until the gills start to get yellow and white stems start turning brown. Place the gills on a paper and rub it with the paper to check the color of the spores. The purple spores appear, leaving a spore print. Check the mycelium; it will have blue bruises. Take a closer look at the edges of the gills and you will notice a white-colored band around it. If the mushrooms have all these characteristics at once, then they are from the psilocybe genus.

For further confirmation, you can also use a laboratory test to check the presence of psilocybe and psilocin. This technique will surely help to identify the psilocybin mushrooms. However, practice makes a person an expert in something, so don't trust your first observation for identification. Both techniques, like bluing reactions and spore printing, requires deep observations. If a person has good observation, he can become a Psilocybe identifier in a short time.

Impact of Psilocybin Mushrooms on Other Plants and Animals

Impact on Plants

Psilocybin mushrooms are saprotrophs; therefore, they will have their impacts on other plants and animals wherever they grow. If we talk about the effects of Psilocybin mushrooms on other plants, it is not a major concern as these mushrooms are fungi, they cannot make their own food like usual plants. They depend on other living organisms for their food by degrading the grass or plants on which they grow, most of the times. But sometimes, they provide protection to the plants near to where they grow from insects and animals. When the animal or insect who tries to eat the plant, near to the place where the psilocybin mushrooms are growing, the animal or insect can accidentally eat the mushroom, which gives the message to an animal to not eat the plant. Thus, psilocybin mushrooms can play a role as plant savers. These mushrooms also grow in gardens and grasslands. The food cycle continues as it is a natural system.. Plants and psilocybin mushrooms are actually close relatives. However, the nature of mushrooms is different from plants because plants can make their own food while fungi cannot make their own food.

Impact on Animals

A report was expressed in 2010 that TV actress Alexandra's goats, which were present in a sanctuary, accidentally ate psilocybin mushrooms and they got lethargic. The goats vomited and showed mental retardation at that time but recovered after two days. Before that, in 2009, BBC showed a documentary about a Siberian reindeer that they felt showed effects of psilocybin mushrooms. These reindeer seem to enjoy eating those magic mushrooms. The Siberian mystics sometimes used to drink the urine of reindeer, which has effects of psilocybin mushrooms to get the hallucinogenic effects during some religious rituals.

Animals that eat Psilocybin mushrooms also face hallucinogenic effects. Scientists and researchers can use these effects for their own purposes. They also vomit and show sickness; sometimes, the animal may die if it has eaten these mushrooms in large quantities. In short words, these psilocybin mushrooms, having hallucinogenic properties and should be away from the access of animals, especially dairy animals. If dairy animals eat those mushrooms, the effect of the hallucinogenic characteristics travels through the milk and urine, and badly affect the human mental condition. Animals also play an important part in the dispersal of these psilocybin mushrooms. Animal manure may prove itself as the best substrate for the growth of Psilocybin mushrooms. Not only the substrate, but it is also a source of dispersal of spores because psilocybin mushrooms grow on heaps, grasslands, etc., thus it is necessary to identify the mushrooms before their cultivation.

Why They Are Magic Mushrooms

Why are these mushrooms called magic mushrooms? Their magical properties are the reasons which lead to their use in rituals and religious ceremonies. The priests and mystics believed that these mushrooms have spiritual effects on the human brain. Therefore, many people started to worship these mushrooms because they thought that it has powers gifted by God or some spiritual powers. All these things are mentioned before in history etc. When science progressed, scientists and researchers started searching on Psilocybin mushrooms to find the mystery behind their magical properties. The research showed that these mushrooms were not magical and were not hallucinogenic long before. They got magical properties and hallucinogenic compounds by evolution.

There were lots of these mysterious mushrooms and insects used to come and eat them. Psilocybin mushrooms, like other organisms, developed such properties to protect themselves from insects. These mushrooms got Psilocybin and Psilocin compounds from the environment. The adaptation of these compounds was then in the genes of those mushrooms. Mushrooms got the genes of Psilocybin and Psilocin by horizontal gene transfer, thus gaining the hallucinogenic properties, and therefore called magic mushrooms. The psilocybin mushrooms developed the power when insects came near or tried to eat them; mushrooms altered the insect's mind, and the insects decide it is in their best interest to leave the mushroom as it is, refusing to consume it. This is the property that many organisms adapt to protect themselves from predators. We can say that mushrooms became Psilocybin mushrooms for their survival.

Scientists kept on researching on these mushrooms and their compounds. They are called magic mushrooms because they alter the minds and put some magical effects on the brain. Scientists and mycologists are still searching on different species of magic mushrooms. These can play an important role in treating different mental disorders, as depicted by the research. As these mushrooms alter the working ability of the brain in insects, it can also put some magical effects on the human brain. The compound Psilocybin has been studied for its use in the treatment of mental disorders. So, Psilocybin mushrooms can be used as a treatment of chronic depression and anxiety. It has been studied that the compounds psilocybin and psilocin present in these mushrooms have the ability to pull out the negative thoughts from the mind, hence the reason they can be helpful in the treatment of many mental disorders.

What Is Magical in These Mushrooms

These mushrooms have been successfully used in some mental therapies due to its components. The psychedelic compounds in these mushrooms were tested on patients with mental disorders. The results of the data obtained showed that those patients expressed positive changes in their attitude. The research reported that those patients treated with Psilocybin mushrooms were found to be closer to nature after treatment. Even they changed their religious and political points of view. Psychedelic research group (PRG), performed research by hiring volunteers having depression (which showed resistance to treatment). They were given oral Psilocybin (extracted from Psilocybin mushrooms), and they were also provided with little counseling during the research. Then a paper was published in this research in the Journal of Psychopharmacology. The research showed that the patients were connected more to nature, and their political views were also changed. It clearly depicts the strong connection of Psilocybin mushrooms modifying brain activities and thoughts.

This natural substance which changed the human mind in lesser time is considered strange. Researchers and scientists are still working on these mushrooms to find the exact phenomena on which these Psilocybin mushrooms work to create hallucinations. These mushrooms have a good taste, but when animals or insects eat them, it acts with the neurotransmitters of the animals — thus altering their nervous system. This is the phenomenon that makes these mushrooms magical, and that's the reason that mystics used them in their rituals and performances.

The Short Biological Properties of Psilocybin Mushrooms

Biological properties of Psilocybin mushrooms, extracted by the research are:

- Psilocybin mushrooms became hallucinogenic and magic mushrooms by horizontal gene transfer thousands of years ago.
- They have slightly different looks as compared to other mushrooms, but their identification is only possible with high expertise.
- The life cycle of Psilocybin mushrooms is the same as other mushrooms, and they are saprotrophs.
- Other animals and plants are affected positively or negatively by the presence of these psilocybin mushrooms .
- They used to grow in grasslands, gardens, animal dung, and in some disturbed habitats.
- The hallucinogenic properties of these mushrooms have made them unique.
- They come under the category of edible mushrooms, but not as a food, but as a medicine
- In many countries, the cultivation of Psilocybin mushrooms is not legal due to its drug-like properties.
- Psilocybe is grouped as Drug 1 category, because it puts hallucinogenic effects on the human mind.
- A person feels nausea after eating hallucinogenic mushrooms.
- These mushrooms like to grow in dark and humid places, therefore, old mushrooms are found in caves.

Their spores allow them to make themselves easily dormant when the conditions are inappropriate.

CHAPTER FOUR

Properties of Psilocybin mushrooms

Magic mushrooms first evolved by the effects of the environment. The changes in climate and environment bring changes in the behavior of Magic mushrooms. The main factors affecting these mushrooms include humidity, soil conditions, resource competition, disease impact, and surrounding predators. Predators, like insects, have been a major factor in bringing changes in Psilocybin mushrooms. The environment also affects how the magic mushrooms grow and the number of chemicals they have. As mentioned earlier, the major compounds present in magic mushrooms are Psilocybin and Psilocin. There are some other chemical compounds in magic mushrooms, including norpsilocin, baeicystin, norbaeocystin, and aeruginascin. It is not necessary that all the compounds are present in equal amounts in all parts of the mushrooms. Different parts contain different amounts of these chemicals. The highest amount of Psilocybin is present in the fruiting body when the caps of *Panaeolus Subalteatus* were studied for chemical properties. There is a difference between the chemical properties of wild and cultivated mushrooms. The wild mushrooms show high variabilities in the chemical compounds they contain. The reason is, wild mushrooms have vast habitats, and they can grow in many different places, even in caves. While cultivated, mushrooms have only a few major chemical compounds because they are grown under controlled conditions at specific places.

Chemical Properties of Wild Magic Mushrooms

The chemical properties of wild magic mushrooms can be studied by taking a look at previous research. Two mycologists and researchers, Bigwood and Beug, in 1982 observed the tenfold difference in the chemical properties of wild and cultivated mushrooms. A study was conducted on 52 samples of wild *Psilocybe semilanceata*, collected from Switzerland. These samples were collected in 5 years. In all these samples, the content of Psilocin in samples varied from 0.21 to 2.02%, while the content of baeocystine varied from 0.05% to 0.77%. The researchers concluded this difference due to the time and age of mushrooms, their size, and fruiting body part differences were responsible for these differences in chemical composition. Another interesting and important thing is, dried mushrooms contain more psilocybin in simple words, less mass and more psilocybin. This is the reason that dried mushrooms are illegal to use in many countries because of their wrong uses as drug. Look at table 4.1, showing the chemical composition of some important psilocybin mushrooms.

Species	Psilocybin	Psilocin	Baeocystin
P. azurescens	1.78	0.38	0.35
P. bohemica	1.34	0.11	0.02
P. baeocystis	0.85	0.59	0.1
P. tampanensis	0.68	0.32	n/a
P. hoogshagenii	0.6	0.1	n/a
P. stuntzii	0.36	0.12	0.02

Table 4.1: the amount of some compounds in %

Chemical Properties of Cultivated Magic Mushrooms

The work of Bigwood and Beug is very useful in understanding the differences in the properties of wild and cultivated Psilocybin mushrooms. They observed a big difference in the chemical content of wild and cultivated magic mushrooms. *Psilocybe cubensis,* when grown on rye grain, showed different chemical properties than the wild *Psilocybe cubensis.* There was also a difference in amounts of Psilocybin and Psilocin. In the fruiting bodies of *Psilocybe cubensis,* there was no Psilocin at the first harvesting period. While its level became high in the fourth harvest, there was no change in the amount of Psilocybin in all harvesting periods, which is always higher than the level of Psilocin.

Gartz and his team, in 1989, cultivated mushrooms and grew them on cow dung-rice growing medium. When they increased the amount of Tryptamine, the psilocin content was increased from 0.09% to 3.3%. Their experiments revealed that the magic mushrooms grown on tryptamine enriched media contain a less amount of Psilocybin as compared to Psilocin.

Chemical and Physical Properties of Psilocybin

Psilocybin is water containing a crystalline compound. It is sometimes recrystallized from water. The soft, white colored crystalline needles, containing water, is an actual form of Psilocybin. This compound melts at 220 to 280 degrees. Psilocybin is 20 parts water, but if we dissolve it in methanol, it is soluble in 120 parts of methanol. In boiling methanol, thick prisms of Psilocybin are produced, which then form crystal methanol, the melting temperature of this crystal is 185 go 195 degrees. If someone wants to put the compound in some insoluble solution, then use chloroform and benzene. The solubility of Psilocybin is very poor in ethanol, according to experiments.

The Psilocin is actually the degradation product of Psilocybin. When boiled in methanol, the degradation product, Psilocin, forms which is almost insoluble in water, but it is soluble in some organic solvents. These compounds, when isolated by different methods, can be visualized by coupling them with some reagents. The Keller reagent (the iron chloride dissolved and concentrated in acetic acid and sulfuric acid), and the Van-Urk reagent (p-dimethyl benzaldehyde) are two common reagents which can be used to visualize psilocybin and psilocin by coupling. Psilocybin produces violet color while psilocin produces blue color, when they are coupled with reagents. These reactions were discovered by Hofmann and his team in 1958 and 1959. The chemical reactions show that these compounds are also present in nature, other than in Psilocybin mushrooms. We can relate the blue psilocin with the bluing of psilocybin mushrooms when they are picked up. These compounds have high value according to pharmaceutical point of view. The bonds formed by Psilocybin with hydrogen, in other compounds like LSD, can be studied through X-ray crystallography. The melting and boiling points of Psilocybin also depends on the solvent in which they have been dissolved..

The melting and boiling points of Psilocybin come under the category of physical properties, while its reactions and solubility come under the category of chemical properties. For their different purposes, scientists and researchers tried to synthesize the Psilocybin and Psilocin in the laboratory. These compounds can be synthesized in the laboratory as well as can be extracted from Psilocybin mushrooms. To synthesize these compounds, high expertise and understanding of synthesis methods are necessary.

The Chemical Synthesis of Psilocybin and Psilocin

Different methods developed and set by different scientists and researchers.

Method 1:

The chemical synthesis of Psilocybin and Psilocin requires the use of some chemical compounds like indole-3-carbaldehyde. Many researchers reported the methods of chemical synthesis, including Yamada, Shirota, Gathergood, and Scammelis, etc. The protected N-tert butoxycarbonyl -2-indo-3-methoxynate and silyl acetylene can be used for the crystallization of Psilocybin in addition to palladium as a catalyst. Shirorta and his team prepared psilocybin and psilocin on a large scale and synthesized this compound by protecting the hydroxyl group of compounds, 4 acetylindole, which is a commercially available compound. Psilocybin can also be produced by the zwitterion method. These methods can be used to synthesize Psilocybin at large scales.

Method 2:

Method 2 mostly relates to the extraction of Psilocybin and Psilocin from dried mushrooms. First, the Psilocybin was extracted from *Psilocybe Mexicana.* Then, other mushrooms were used for the extraction. When Hofmann and co-workers isolated Psilocybin from *Psilocybe mexicana,* they observed that the substance was dissolved in only polar solvents such as methanol or compound ethanol and water. Psilocin, on the other hand, is easily soluble in low polar solvents such as 1-chlorobutane. Most investigators have used methanol to extract quantities of psilocybin and psilocybin from mushroom samples. Most methods involve mixing fine ground mushroom material with solvents. Extraction time is too high.

Only a few studies have investigated the effect of extraction conditions on recovery from 2 minutes to 24 hours. Perk and his team found that the uniformity of the fine ground samples of Psilocybe *subarginosa* with 30 parts of methanol did not produce maximum production of alkaloids for more than 2 min. This method was found inadequate by a group of researchers when analyzing the specimens of *Psilocybe semilenesta* in Norway. They extracted two samples with ammonium nitrate in methanol in a centrifuge tube, rotating the tubes in a rotary mixer for 30 minutes. Approximate quantitative (98%) yields of Psilocybin were obtained by this method. The role or effect of ammonium nitrate in the extraction solvent was not discussed.

These two methods have been discussed in detail by many scientists and researchers. Let's discuss the molecular structure of Psilocybin.

Molecular Structure of Psilocybin and Psilocin

Psilocybin:

Molecular formula: $C_{12}H_{17}N_{204}P$

Molecular weight: 284.3 g/mol

The molecular structure of Psilocybin looks like:

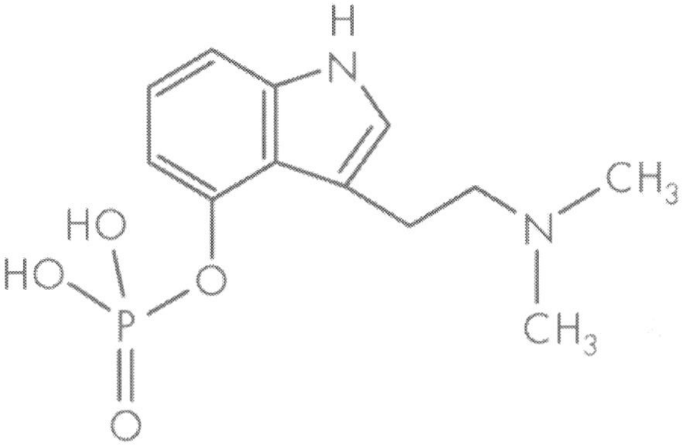

Psilocin

Molecular formula: $C_{12}H_{16}N_{20}$

Molecular weight: 204.3 g/mol

The molecular structure of Psilocin looks like:

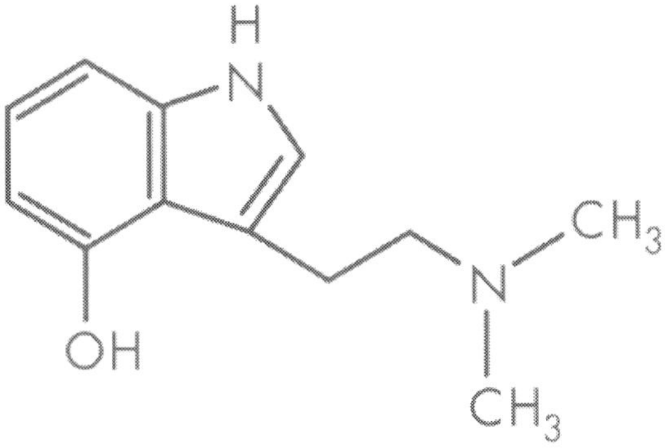

The structure of Psilocybin matches the white crystalline structure of indole. Psilocybin mushrooms contain the ethylamine side chains of different lengths. They also contain tryptamine, so that's the reason when the mushrooms are cultivated on tryptamine enriched mediums, there is less amount of Psilocybin in magic mushrooms. The Psilocybin and Psilocin have resemblance with the chemicals found in the brain. Strangely, the Psilocybin has resemblance with one of the chemicals, the important neurotransmitter found in the brain, serotonin.

Physical and Mental Effects of Psilocybin and Psilocin

The physical and mental effects of psilocybin mushrooms are interesting to discuss. The compounds present in these magic mushrooms, mainly Psilocybin and Psilocin, have amazing effects, depending upon the ingestion. If someone takes a number of magic mushrooms and keeps them in the mouth for 10 to 15 minutes, they start feeling something different. They start having some psycho-activity when swallowed. The effects of taking this amount of Psilocybin mushrooms are yawning, feeling some restlessness, and some bitter taste in the mouth.

Taking any amount of psilocybin mushrooms can cause some physical reactions. Some prompted physical reactions of Psilocybin mushrooms are the dilation of pupils, dry mouth sensation, rise in blood pressure, high rate of heartbeat, high temperature, etc. These effects are due to the inhibition of important neurotransmitters, serotonin. There is a similarity between LSD and Psilocin as they both acts on similar mechanisms.

The physical effects produced by ingesting Psilocybin mushrooms mostly don't happen immediately. It depends on the amount taken in the mouth. The high dose of Psilocybin mushrooms taken in the mouth produces the effects after 8 to 10 minutes and sensations start after 15 to 30 minutes when the chemicals absorb in the stomach wall. They take almost an hour to reach the brain and cross its barriers. When they cross the brain barriers, they start their psychoactivity. The first signs include: yawning, malaise, restlessness. Nausea is also caused by these mushrooms in some people. Mainly, the species *Ps.Caerulescens* and *Ps.Aztecoru* cause severe nausea. Some people feel weakness in the legs, discomfort in the stomach, and chilling effects. These conditions persist for a short time period. After that, most of the people feel physically light and easy. But, in some people, these conditions last for a long time. The studies of the ingestion of Psilocin and Psilocybin in animals showed high doses of these compounds orally. The oral ingestion results in the distribution of these compounds in the whole body. Kidneys get higher concentrations than other body parts.

Biosynthesis of Psilocybin in Magic Mushrooms

There is very little data available on the bio-synthesis of Psilocybin in magic mushrooms. Some authentic studies revealed that there is a structural similarity between Psilocybin, Psilocin, and Tryptophan, so there is a chance that the origin of Psilocybin and Psilocin is amino acid. An experiment was done in 1961 when Brack and his team incorporated Tryptophan in Mycelium cultures of *Psilocybe semperviva* and *Psilocybe cubensis.* To synthesize Psilocybin from Tryptophan, the tryptophan molecule is changed by decarboxylation, methylation of amino group, hydroxylation of the indole moiety present in 4th position, and phosphorylation of 4-hydroxy indole moiety. The order is not necessary, but all these processes are necessary to produce Psilocybin from Tryptophan. It is observed that it is the better precursor of Psilocybin in mushrooms. We can say that the first step in the biosynthesis of Psilocybin from Tryptophan is the decarboxylation of Tryptophan into Tryptamine.

The best precursor of Psilocybin and Psilocin is tryptamine because when it is incorporated into mycelium of a growing mushroom, it develops into good fruiting bodies. *Psilocybe semilanceata* is also able to biosynthesize and bio-transform N-methyltryptamine to 4-phosphoruloxy-N-methyltryptamine.

The Drug-Like Properties

Psilocybin is categorized as a drug, the schedule 1 drug, and it is illegal in many countries. Governments think that this is only a risky compound with zero benefits medically. Psilocybin mushrooms are also known as "shrooms" due to its drug-like properties. A report was released in 2018 in John Hopkins' University, where they said that FDS categorized Psilocybin as a schedule 4 drug now. Drugs like Xanax and Tramadol produce low risk as compared to Psilocybin. In the past few years, a large number of Psilocybin mushrooms was found growing, especially in the UK. So, they warned not to pick this class A drug accidentally. Dried mushrooms were banned already for years. The fresh mushrooms were legal before, but in 2005, these fresh mushrooms also become illegal.

They are illegal in many countries because young people take it as a drug. Mostly, the users of other drugs become addicted to using these mushrooms as drugs. Some people use them with some other compounds like LSD. The use of Psilocybin mushrooms as a drug has got a high percentage in Nordic countries; a report from Denmark showed that. It is considered as a drug due to its hallucinogenic effects, which are produced just after ingestion.

Studies revealed that people who used to eat psilocybin mushrooms, when passed through urinary analysis, showed an amount of psilocybin drug in their urine. The GC-MS analysis methods, when developed, were used to analyze the presence of Psilocin in serum and blood. A study was published in 2004 by Albers and his team, which revealed the presence of Psilocin in blood and serum of people who used to eat psilocybin mushrooms.

Most of the drugs alter the human mind and disturb its focus. Some drugs cause hallucinations, and some put negative thoughts; some drugs disturb the consciousness of a person. Some drugs make a person more active, boost up his neurotransmitters or alter their activities. People start thinking differently by taking some drugs, but when the effects start to fade away, people feel nausea, unconsciousness, body pain, and many other health problems. Psilocybin mushrooms have Psilocybin and Psilocin, as mentioned before, and these compounds are considered as category A drugs.

In many countries, cultivating and eating these mushrooms is illegal. But now, researchers have found some magical properties which can be used as the magical treatments of many mental diseases.

Short Summary

The two major compounds in magic mushrooms, which are responsible for magical and hallucinogenic properties, are Psilocybin and Psilocin. These two compounds have similar chemical and physical properties with slight differences. Mostly, the quantity of Psilocybin is higher than Psilocin. Studies showed that Psilocin is actually a degrading product of Psilocybin; therefore, it is mostly present in low amounts. The synthesis of Psilocybin and Psilocin in laboratories was not possible before due to lack of knowledge and research facilities, but in the 1900s, Hofmann and his team took the first step and synthesized Psilocybin and Psilocin in the laboratory. Isolation of these compounds from mushrooms was already done, which enabled scientists to study their chemical and physical properties in detail. Laboratory synthesis of these two compounds opened the new doors of research, and scientists started studying these compounds in nature. Studies showed that these two compounds are produced due to the presence of their specific genes in Psilocybin mushrooms, and these mushrooms got the genes through horizontal gene transfer.

The chemical and physical properties of Psilocybin mushrooms therefore depend upon the chemical properties of their major compounds, Psilocin and Psilocybin. These two compounds became illegal in many countries, not these compounds, but the cultivation of hallucinogenic mushrooms is also banned in many countries. The reason behind this ban is their drug-like properties. Psilocybin is considered as the A category drug which alters the human mind. Any person who eats the mushrooms or takes the oral dose of Psilocybin feels hallucinations, nausea, and some other physical conditions. Only in few countries, these mushrooms are allowed for research purposes. They are searching to find the treatments of mental disorders with these Psilocybin mushrooms

CHAPTER FIVE

Medicinal Properties of Psilocybin Mushrooms

Psilocybin is a chemical extracted from 100 species of mushrooms that belonged to kingdom fungi. These mushrooms are cultivated as well as grown naturally. Psilocybin is a classic hallucinogen produced in 1958 that was used in spiritual mystic sessions to acquire special connection with spirit. It has medicinal effects used to treat alcoholism, anxiety, obsession and understanding schizophrenia. It is actually a potential psychiatric wonder drug in that period in the '60s. It was used before 1970 as a ritual to reduce depression. The Controlled Substance Act stopped the usage of psilocybin in 1970 in clinical studies using hallucinogens and psychedelics. Research on theses agent mostly was completed in the 1950s and 1960s, but it was not taken seriously because of the small nature of studies lack of professionalism and incompetence with current research standards. If studies on this had not been stopped, we might get a lot of wonders in the medical field. We can recreate new ways to treat mental illnesses and other life-threatening diseases. It can lead to the discovery of neurotransmitters and can calm down nervousness, sleeplessness and anxiety. It's probably a dedicated chemical to use as an antidepressant, which can help to solve the mental crisis. The National Institute on Drug Abuse, Food and Drug Administration advisory committee allowed resumption of research on psychedelics agents in 1992. It changed the perception of drug.

Biological Impacts

Psilocybin mushrooms, as shown by their name, are known for the presence of alkaloid compound psilocybin. Psilocybin has very strong **hallucinogenic effects**, so these mushrooms, if ingested, affect your body's metabolism to a great level. As soon as psilocybin enters the body, it is converted after metabolism into another compound known as psilocin, which starts to bring changes in the nervous system that induces hallucination. (Hallucination is a delusional state of mind in which a person sees or hears vivid things without any external stimulus). Psilocin is the primary psychoactive substance present in psychedelic mushrooms. It (psilocybin) produces the same effects as produced by other drugs like **mescaline** and **LSD** (lysergic acid Diethylamide). This is not life-threatening usually but, due to its strong hallucinogenic characteristics, it may produce very unpleasant effects like other hallucinogenic substances. However, there are some risks that are specifically related to mushrooms. The biological impacts of magic mushrooms can be seen physically just after the intake, but these mushrooms also produce alteration at cell or tissue level, and these internal effects may not be felt at once but appear later with the passage of time.

Physical Effects

The physical effects of psychedelic mushrooms are,

- Dizziness
- Increased heartbeat
- High temperature of the body
- Headache
- Weakness in muscles and body
- Increased blood pressure
- Sleepiness

Mental Effects:

- Euphoria
- Auditory or visual Hallucination
- Neuropsychiatric instability
- Distortion in sensory perceptions
- Paranoia
- Psychosis
- Panic reactions

Overall Biological Effects:

Some biological impacts are some symptoms that appear immediately or slowly after ingesting psychedelic mushrooms:

- Psilocybin attacks the parts of the brain that are associated with emotions like fear, rage, anxiety, etc. and develop stress and **anxiety.**

- Panic attacks are also observed after intake of psilocybin.
- The person feels detached and is surrounded by negative feelings and **impaired judgment** etc.
- If some wrong type of mushroom is ingested mistakenly, then it may cause severe poisoning and even death.
- **HPPD** (Hallucinogen Persistent Perpetual Disorder) can also occur in which there are flashbacks or reoccurrence of the effects caused by psilocybin long after the intake. Such a condition can be very unpleasant and distressing.

The National Institute on Drug Abuse illustrates all properties and biological impacts of every kind of hallucinogenic chemicals and drugs, including the psilocybin mushrooms that are also being abused for hallucinogenic and euphoric effects. According to this institute, the psilocybin mushrooms induce hallucination by passing through the **neural pathways** and acts on the frontal lobe of the forebrain cortex (that is primarily responsible for the actions and responses associated with vision, hearing, and smelling).

The compound psilocin performs its function by acting on the sensory parts of the brain with the help of the neurotransmitter serotonin. The action of psilocybin on the nervous system is not temporary; rather, it produces many long-lasting changes in physical as well as mental health. These changes are either positive or negative, depending upon the method of use, potency, and activity of psilocybin, the quantity of psilocybin, and the frequency of its intake.

Pharmacological Importance of Psilocybin Mushrooms:

Psilocybin is an alkaloid compound that has the potential to alter the brain activities; its isolation was first done (by Albert Hofmann) from a mushroom *psilocybe mexicana,* found in Central America. When it is converted into its pharmacologically active form, i.e., psilocin, it acts directly on sensory areas of thalamus in the human brain. Psilocin primarily reduces or suppresses thalamic activity and consequently helps in reducing stress and depression. Psilocybin produces a strong physiological response at 5-HT (2A), whose receptors are located in the thalamus and cortex of the brain, and produces a moderate physiological response at 5-HT (2A) and 5-HT (2C). These responses alter sensory perceptions in the thalamus and consequently cause hallucinations. When psilocybin is given to the body, it starts its action in about 20 to 40 minutes and remains for 3 to 6 hours.

This is an addictive drug, so that's why magic mushrooms are illegal to use directly as they are also being used in drug abuse that has many lethal effects on human health as well as the society. Even the clinical studies and experiments on hallucinogens and psychedelics were restricted in 1970 in accordance with the Control Substance Act (**CSA**). But, as years passed, the significance of the neuropsychiatric effects of these agents and their strong therapeutic abilities was realized, and the need for analytical study and research in this field was understood. Then the National Institute on Drug Abuse took under consideration all medical and clinical aspects of hallucinogens and psychedelics, so they allowed all research work and study on these chemicals to begin in 1992.

Now, they are legal to be used as a source of medicines to extract psilocybin and other chemicals of medical and economic importance from them, and they proved to be really useful in the field of pharmaceutics and medicine. It is largely used in pharmaceutical industries in the manufacture of a number of medicines. Due to its hallucinogenic and suppressive activity, psilocybin is used in medicines that are particularly related to nervous disorders. Psilocybin is metabolized to psilocin, which goes to neural highways (5-HT pathways) and acts to decrease the stress and anxiety. Nowadays, depression and anxiety are increasing to an alarming level, so several medicines are now being manufactured to cure anxiety-related disease and depression. Psilocybin is added in an appropriate ratio according to the requirement of the medicine for a particular disorder.

Hallucinogenic Effects of Psychedelic Mushrooms:

Hallucination is a delusional state of mind that may be auditory or visual in which the sufferer hears or sees the things which do not exist in actual. Hallucination is triggered by several nervous disorders like Parkinson's disease, schizophrenia, brain tumor, and also by severe diseases of kidney and liver. It also occurs with the use of addictive drugs, such as marijuana, heroin, alcohol, cocaine, and nicotine. Psilocybin performs the main action on the nervous system and causes drowsiness and hallucination just as done by LSD and mescaline, but it has less hallucinogenic properties than these strong hallucinogenic drugs.

When the psilocybin from the magic mushrooms gets into the blood of a person, a metabolism takes place, which converts it into another substance, psilocin. Psilocin goes directly to the nervous system through blood circulation and starts its job as a psychoactive agent. It makes the user suffer from all those conditions that are caused by addictive drugs for example,

- bad trips
- Dizziness
- Unconsciousness
- delayed headache
- nausea
- drowsiness
- diarrhea
- muscle weakness and pain
- anxiety
- fear or rage
- psychosis

All these conditions arise from the excessive intake of psilocybin. The exact situation of the psilocybin user and the immediately appeared symptoms depend on the dose of psilocybin consumed by that person. Sometimes, a small dose does not have many negative effects, and also, they do not remain for a longer period of time to affect the body's health to a dangerous level.

But, if psilocybin is consumed frequently or taken in a large amount at one time, it may prove lethal to health. More quantity of psilocybin causes intense neurological and psychiatric disorders such as:

- The patient may go in a state of coma for a long time.
- Intense level of stress and anxiety
- Paranoia
- Hallucination and poor brain function
- Seizures
- Depression
- Vomiting and other digestive disorders

Psychedelics produce a number of long-term effects on the entire body of the consumer. Magic mushrooms were banned and were illegal to cultivate due to these hallucinogenic and also addictive properties as people can abuse them. A person may become dependent on it and subjected to severe panic conditions, least tolerance, and negative emotional changes.

Medical Uses

Besides having negative impacts on human health, psilocybin mushrooms also play a positive role in the medical treatments because of their magical properties. The medical treatment of certain ailments involving the use of psilocybin extracted from the psychedelic or psilocybin mushrooms is now getting popular and is known as "Psilocybin therapy." Psilocybin, the main effective ingredient of magic mushrooms, plays a great therapeutic role in the cure of many diseases; thus, it's a worthy topic of discussion and practice in the field of medicine. As the research and studies on magic mushrooms began, its first use was made to treat anxiety and associated disorders. Psilocybin mushrooms are significantly helpful in treating the stressful situations that arise in a patient when he/she is suffering from a chronic disease like:

- Cancer in any part of the body
- Trauma or injury due to some accident
- Some severe viral or bacterial infection
- Physiological or physical disorder.
- A serious distressing condition can also occur due to acute pain after a surgery
- Any irritation or panic attack during or after a treatment that involves frequent injections, stitches, high potency medicines, etc.

In such cases, psilocybin proves really helpful to relieve stress and pain. The dosage of psilocybin given to a patient is also very important for getting the required results in the treatment. It is usually given in the form of an oral capsule that contains 200mcg (given per kg weight of the patient) active psilocybin or 250mg niacin. Niacin is used as a control by scientists as it produces a warm flushing effect in the body; this is a common adverse effect of psilocybin, without producing an alteration in the brain or psychological state. It has been subjected to a number of experiments and was given to the patients at regular intervals (mostly 2 weeks) to prove its remedial abilities and found it to be remarkably effective in reducing anxiety. This therapeutic role of psilocybin is confirmed by different **research institutes,** for example, National Institute on Drug Abuse, Emma Sofia in Norway, Multidisciplinary Association for Psychedelic Studies (MAPS) in California, The Kings College London and the Heffter Research Institute in America.

Psilocybin works with the blood flow in the nervous tissues of the body. An experiment was done to see the role of psilocybin in reducing stress and anxiety by comparing the **MRI reports on cerebral blood flow** before and after a regular dose of psilocybin. It was observed that psilocybin decreases the blood circulation in those sensory areas of the brain, which are responsible for producing stress and anxiety. The most effective results of psilocybin therapy are seen after one week.

Psilocybin therapy is performed in a single session or a series of sessions at regular intervals, depending upon the severity of the medical issue and particular biological conditions of the patient. But, in most cases, a single session of psilocybin therapy is effective enough to give long-term cure to the patient.

Safety

Psilocybin has similar effects to lysergic acid diethylamide (LSD) and mescaline, but psilocybin is not addictive in nature: patients can easily stop its usage. Studies on a group of people showed that patients were safe from drug abuse, persisting perception disorders, prolonged psychosis, or other long-term deficits in functioning. The adverse effect of psilocybin was reported very few and mostly related to high doses. Experimental groups were observed for 8 months after the administration of the drug (psilocybin) and no harsh side effects were observed. People from the psilocybin administered group were calm and peaceful during all the experimental conduct. There have been some concerns regarding the use of psychedelics agents that they may cause mental retardation and cause an attempt of suicide among people who used them. A study conducted on people to observe those effects does not support the above claim. No significant relation was found between the use of psilocybin and mental retardation or suicidal thoughts, attempts or plans. It is the safest drug out there. For example, in 2018, just 0.3 % of people who reported taking them needed medical emergency treatment

Release Depressed Mood Swings

Studies showed that use of psilocybin could reduce anxiety suicidal thoughts and depression. The study was conducted using data from the national survey on drug use and health. They divided the participants into four groups who used psilocybin; only one used psilocybin with psychedelics, while the other was non- psilocybin psychedelics only and one group which used none of them in their entire life. Results shocked all the odds and myths against psilocybin. They were quite progressive and satisfactory about the use of psilocybin. The group that used psilocybin showed less distress and disappointment as compared to the other groups. They appear far better than any others. They showed improvement of moods and stress relief. MRI imaging reveals reduced blood flow in amygdala, a small almond-shaped region of the brain known to balance emotional responses, sleep-wake cycle and thinking process in humans. People started to take minor doses of it; they think it can improve their insight, perception of understanding of others, enhance a person's capacity for self-transcendence, which is needed to overcome self-deception. *It can make you more attentive and able to focus problems.* From the results, scientists conclude that psilocybin may play a role in decreasing anxiety, mood swing and bring peace in people's behaviors. Some treatments for mental health and care suggest the use of psilocybin. In certain cases, extreme use of this chemical may cause vomiting, nausea and hallucination, but this happens in rare cases with psilocybin abuse.

Tobacco Cessation

Psilocybin has a high affinity for several serotonin receptors like 5-HT_{1A}, 5-HT_{2A}, and 5-HT_{2C}, which located in numerous areas of the brain, including the cerebral cortex and thalamus.

Studies have shown positive evidence that use of 5-HT_{2A}O receptor agonist is helpful in the treatment of addiction. Research was conducted on 15 participants enrolled in a smoking cessation course that includes administration of psilocybin in their therapy period at weeks 5,7 and 13. All other medications were stopped for those patients. They smoked 10 cigarettes per day. Cognitive-behavioral therapy had been done for a 4-week period while using cigarettes. The study revealed positive effects of smoking prohibition on patients. The group of people using psilocybin stopped smoking at the 6th week of study. This shows that psilocybin has a magical effect of releasing any kind of addiction. It is the best sensational drug to stop smoking among patients taking vernicles.

Psychological Effects

It has a calming effect; it also has a pathogen effect similar to MDMA, a helpful and beneficial compound in reducing stress and making good perception about problems and people. Psilocybin converted into psilocin which binds to serotonin receptor called 2A, and experts think that's what triggers what they call neuronal avalanching. It can cause different changes in the brain and you have increased activity in the cortex which leads to change in perception. There is also decreased network activity in the default mode network, which leads to loss of ego and that's why people report a profound sense of unity transcending beyond themselves. Psilocybin increases connectivity among different parts of the brain. Due to this receptor activation, different areas of the brain synchronize with each other like an orchestra. Once psilocybin enters, it coordinates and communicates all parts of the brain, also those parts which are normally compartmentalized and doing their own work. Scientists believe that it's a combination of these effects that makes psilocybin useful for combating addiction and depression. When new areas or region in the brain start talking to each other, it can be profound. Healing can be helpful in the thought process and give a critical analysis of problems. Despite all benefits, psilocybin is still listed as a Schedule I drug, a category reserved for compounds that have currently accepted no medical use.

Obsessive-Compulsive Disorder

A study has reviewed the potential benefits of psilocybin on obsessive-compulsive disorder. It is a mental health disorder that affected people of all ages and every field; it occurs when a person gets caught in a cycle of obsessions and compulsions. This can affect the prefrontal cortex. Patient with OCD found that prefrontal cortex gets relieved after the few weeks of usage. It is safer than alcohol, tobacco, cannabis, and is non-addictive. Studies showed a positive effect of psilocybin on this disorder. People who suffered from this disorder get rid of disease while using psilocybin. A study conducted on 9 patients with OCD, to check the impact of psilocybin mushrooms. They hypothesized that the oral administration of psilocybin would reduce the effects of OCD. Before the experiment, those patients tried the treatment for the disease.

Patients were given four different doses at least for one week. From among all the population, 88.9% of people showed a decreased effect of the symptoms.

Alcohol Dependence

Psilocybin is a magical drug used in mental health care. Its high affinity for serotonin 2A receptors in the brain will reduce addiction of many kinds. It can be helpful for people struggling with alcohol addiction. This is also proved through cognitive study. These are natural hallucinogens that is structurally similar to serotonin and DMT. Psilocin is an active biological form of psilocybin. There is a long history of the usage of psilocybin as a therapy for alcohol addiction. Now, in the current study conducted on that, people reported a very positive effect of psilocybin on alcoholism treatment. They reported mystical transforming experiences.

Anxiety Disorder

In the society we are living today, we need consistent fixers for our deep-rooted problems. From pharmaceutical medication to anti-depressant to antipsychotic meds, we are looking for a quick solution to bandage our sufferings. Results of these medicines may be quick, but they can affect people in many other ways. They can lead to long-term conflictions with existing problems. What if I can tell you a better alternative? These are the magic mushrooms from the backyard of your garden. These mushrooms have been used for thousands of years for almost every field.

Anxiety is an emotional feeling characterized by stress and tension. Different factors can increase anxiety in a person like the failure of losing something feeling to get success in life. Some patients with chronic and life-threatening diseases also suffer from anxiety like cancer. Studies revealed psilocybin reduced anxiety among cancer patients when administered with successive control dosage of psilocybin. Psilocybin can be used as a medication for the management of anxiety disorders. Magic mushrooms cure neurological disorders like PTSD, depression, OCD over active amygdale and migraines. Magic mushroom may reset the activity of the brain circuit known to play a role in depression. Use of magic mushroom can bring a very beautiful feeling. It has healing powers and has been used from many thousands of years to bring unity and enlightenment.

Cancer Therapy

Psilocybin has been used in rituals for centuries. Modern study revealed the medicinal effect of psilocybin in cancer treatment. Cancer is a life-threatening disease. Patients lose their all hopes for life; they go into a critical condition obsessed with dark thoughts. This negative approach of patients may adversely affect the immune system of the patient, which is already compromised. In some cases, the patient collapses due to the stress of the disease. Here, psilocybin again saves them from depression and anxiety. It can save a struggling patient's life. Its effect on the serotonin receptors reduces depression.

Reported by Johns Hopkins, upcoming studies will evaluate the use of psilocybin as a new therapy for opioid addiction, Alzheimer's disease, post-traumatic stress disorder (PTSD), post-treatment Lyme disease syndrome (formerly known as chronic Lyme disease), anorexia nervosa and alcohol use in people with major depression. A focus on precision medicine tailored to the individual patient is expected.

However, even if approved by the FDA, psilocybin would have to be reclassified by the DEA to schedule II substance for it to be available for patients.

Conclusion

We can conclude from the above discussion that psilocybin is helpful in convulsive retarding behaviors. We have observed a reduction in different mental health illnesses, anxiety, emotional disturbance addiction, alcohol dependence and effective for cancer patients. Results were received on a specific population, so fluctuations can be expected while studying them on a large population. The study has limitations. As current studies are mostly limited to case reports, open-label trials, retrospective studies, larger or more robust studies should be conducted with this agent to determine the real impact and clinical utility for each disease state. Some ingredients in the magic mushroom relieve the pain and distress. This will bring some meaning and hope to the people. The substances are not to be taken lightly due to its vast effects. Ranging from neurological disorders or pain management they have a great influence on pharmacopoeia. What do you think they should prescribe medically or not?

Mushrooms are not new in the human diet; they were used by indigenous people long times ago. Humans used to eat mushrooms even at the time when they didn't know their names. They were not only part of dishes but also the part of religious and cultural rituals. But mushrooms are not only edibles, but they are also death caps and death angles as well as hallucinogens. There are thousands of mushrooms in the world which belong to the kingdom fungi. Some of the species of fungi are too diverse that they don't match a single morphological feature with each other. Mushrooms are actually fruiting bodies of fungi, which are diverse in shape and nature. Edible mushrooms are even different in taste: some are normal, and some are very delicious. Hallucinogenic mushrooms belong to the order Agaricales of basidiomycetes. Almost all classes of order Agaricales are Psilocybin mushrooms, containing hallucinogenic properties. Psilocybin mushrooms are those which contain two specific psychoactive compounds which are also used in some drugs. This book is about Psilocybin mushrooms; therefore, the evolution, occurrences, and other properties of these mushrooms have been discussed in earlier chapters.

Short Summary

The Psilocybin mushrooms are more than hallucinogenic. They have many positive effects on mental and physical health when they are used in controlled doses. Due to ban on these mushrooms in some countries, the research process stopped. But, many countries, when they realized the importance of Psilocybin mushrooms, allowed their cultures to grow in labs and also allowed researchers to collect these mushrooms. They are very different from other species of fungi, especially due to the presence of Psilocybin and psilocin. These two compounds are responsible for all the uniqueness of Psilocybin mushrooms. These mushrooms have many neurological and psychological effects on the human mind. Therefore, psychiatrists now prefer to use these mushrooms as antidepressants. Their pharmacological and pharmaceutical uses are also unlimited as the pharmacists are using these mushrooms in different medicines. The research on these mushrooms has revealed that they are important and beneficial, but one must follow safety instructions about these mushrooms. High doses of Psilocybin mushrooms can lead to death. Unconditional exposure to Psilocybin is also dangerous for health.

Chapter six

Legality of Psilocybin Mushrooms Around the World

The major compounds present in Psilocybin mushrooms are Psilocybin and Psilocin. These two compounds are considered a drug like controlled substances and categorized under Schedule 1 drug. It was categorized in schedule 1 in a convention on Psychotropic substances in 1971. The control of these substances is different in different countries. In some countries of Europe, the mushrooms containing these substances are totally banned. While in some countries there is a ban on just these compounds, not on mushrooms. Some countries have a partial ban; for example, the fresh mushrooms are allowed while dried, and processed psilocybin mushrooms are illegal. There are some countries where the cultivation and production of Psilocybin mushrooms are totally allowed - even the production of Psilocybin and Psilocin are also legal. The countries where Psilocybin mushrooms are illegal, consider these mushrooms as a drug. While the countries which have allowed the legal cultivation of these mushrooms think that these mushrooms can be helpful in some research.

In some of the countries, the permission of cultivation of Psilocybin mushrooms is given depending upon the intention of growth of these mushrooms. Like, if someone is asking for psilocybin mushroom cultivation for the research purpose, he will be given permission by the government. Thus, in some countries, it is legal depending upon the intentions behind their growth. In some countries, Psilocybin itself is illegal but the Psilocybin mushrooms legal.

Countries Where Psilocybin Mushrooms Are Legal

Jamaica is a small country, where a number of Psilocybin mushroom species have found. In this small country, the use, selling, transport, possession, everything is legal about Magic mushrooms. In Jamaica, magic mushrooms are also known as "Shrooms."

There is a restriction on selling and transport of magic mushrooms in the **British Virgin Islands**. Although the possession, cultivation and personal use of these mushrooms are allowed in the country, but selling and transport are not legal. Still, vendors are seen selling these mushrooms to tourists without understanding the results of breaking the law.

Brazil is a country where the production, possession, personal use and general consumption of Psilocybin mushroom. There is nothing in their law about the illegal use of Psilocybin mushrooms and activities related to them. The substance Psilocybin itself is not legal, but Psilocybin mushrooms are totally legal and allowed.

In some countries, like the **Netherlands**, Psilocybin mushrooms are illegal, but there is a part of the law in which the cultivation of magic mushrooms is allowed. Truffle is a developmental stage in Psilocybin mushrooms. Psilocybin mushrooms are not allowed to grow completely in the **Netherlands**, but the cultivation of Psilocybin mushrooms is allowed. This part, truffle also contains large amounts of Psilocybin.

Austria allows the use of Psilocybin but for a good purpose. If you are using or growing Psilocybin mushrooms in Austria, you have to provide an explanation to why you are using these mushrooms and what's your intention to use them. They are legal until you don't ingest them, and you just use them for research and good purposes.

In **Canada**, magic mushrooms are almost illegal, but you can buy and sell their spores and can also use microdoses of these mushrooms. Cultivation of Psilocybin mushrooms is not allowed as it goes against the Canadian law, because the production of the substance "Psilocybin" is prohibited,

Czech Republic allows the use of Psilocybin mushrooms, in small quantities. Large amounts of Psilocybin mushrooms are illegal. The production is allowed, but the purpose should not be the production of substance Psilocybin.

Mexico is a country where a number of Psilocybin species have found. The proper cultivation and growth of Psilocybin mushrooms became illegal in Mexico but after Vienna Convention (held is 1971, in which Psilocybin mushrooms were not considered specifically illegal but the Psilocybin substance is illegal as a drug), the authorities don't keep a check on the production and cultivation of Psilocybin mushrooms. They are allowed for sacramental purposes and for the production of some medicines.

You can have small amounts of magic mushrooms in **Portugal** without going to jail. You can possess these mushrooms and can grow these mushrooms for good purposes, but you are not allowed to use them as a drug. If you are found taking these mushrooms, you will be sent to court-mandated rehabilitation therapy.

In **Spain**, the personal use of magic mushrooms is allowed. But there are no clear laws about the possession of fresh mushrooms; even though there is no clear law about the growing kits and spores.

There are a lot of exceptions in the **United States** around the use of Psilocybin mushrooms. Buying magic mushrooms and their spores are legal in most states of the United States. The spores are allowed if you are not going to grow them. In some states, the use, buying and selling of spores is also illegal; these states include California, Georgia and Idaho. In New Mexico, the Psilocybin Mushrooms are totally allowed and legal. There are religious groups who use these mushrooms for their sacramental uses and rituals. They are also allowed in **Denver** and **Oakland**.

You can see that only a few countries allow these Psilocybin mushrooms completely, but in most of the countries, Psilocybin mushrooms are allowed partially. But still, they are in use, people use them for different purposes. Most of the countries allow the mushrooms, not because of Psilocybin, but because of natural remedies present in them. Most of the countries where they are legally allowed, the buying and selling of these mushrooms are usually for research purposes. Others have made the laws, according to the intentions, for example, if the Psilocybin mushrooms are used for bad intentions, then it is illegal. However, if they are used for good intentions, then they are legal.

Countries Where Psilocybin Mushrooms Are Illegal

Psilocybin mushrooms are found naturally in many regions of the world. But they are not legal for use in many countries of the world. For example, in the **United Kingdom**, every type of use of Psilocybin mushrooms, their cultivation, buying and selling everything is illegal. You will be considered to be involved in drug dealings if you are found having these mushrooms. It is because it is considered a drug.

In many countries of **Asia, including India, Bangladesh, Pakistan, China, Malaysia, Indonesia, Iran**, and many others, the use, buying, selling, spore dealing and the likes are not allowed. It is considered an illegal drug in these countries. We can say that except the countries mentioned in the above section, all countries have banned the use of Psilocybin mushrooms for ingestion and cultivation purpose. But, in some countries, there are no clear laws about the use and misuse of Psilocybin mushrooms. For example, in Afghanistan, there is no clear law about these mushrooms. There is no natural growth of these mushrooms in Afghanistan, and there is no legal paper about these mushrooms in Afghanistan.

They are illegal in many countries; still, if some people find them, they may use them for their purposes. Scientists are always in search of new topics for research, so they are successfully doing research on Psilocybin mushrooms, but people who have no relationship with science may use these mushrooms illegally at home. Many countries, just perceive Psilocybin mushrooms as a source of Psilocybin and Psilocin, and these two compounds have drug-like properties. Therefore they consider Psilocybin mushrooms as alternatives of drugs.

Legal Alternatives of Magic Mushrooms

If someone wants to grow and use Psilocybin mushrooms, but their country doesn't allow them, they can still get these mushrooms and can use these mushrooms for their good purpose.

Many countries, allow the spores of Psilocybin mushrooms even if they are not allowing the cultivation of these mushrooms. You can then purchase spores and grow kits. You can also buy Psilocybin mushrooms, magic mushrooms in some countries and can ship them to other countries. There is a chemical named 4-AcO-DMT, which is allowed in many countries. This chemical is known to reduce or change the effects of Psilocybin. But, don't purchase chemical from anyone, only use chemical from trusted companies. Magic mushrooms are the only legal alternative of Psilocybin mushrooms in the countries where the production and use of these mushrooms are not allowed.

Spores can also be an alternative of Psilocybin mushrooms because people can use these spores to cultivate mushrooms in their homes. Although cultivation is not allowed in many countries, but if you are growing a small amount of these mushrooms using their spores, and you have no bad intentions, then there will be no problem with the cultivation.

How Psilocybin and Psilocybin Mushrooms Are Sold

Psilocybin mushrooms are used by many people despite the restrictions and specific laws. People who know the benefits of Psilocybin mushrooms always look for its doses. They can be used in medicines of anxiety and depression, which help to reduce the conditions. They are also used for complete treatment of many mental disorders. Some researchers grow these mushrooms on small levels to meet their research requirements while some people grow them at large scales for other purposes. Large scale production of Psilocybin mushrooms is allowed in some regions.

All the disputes of Psilocybin mushrooms are due to their hallucinogenic properties due to the presence of Psilocybin compound in Psilocybin mushrooms. So, the compounds Psilocybin and Psilocin are considered hallucinogenic and magic compounds due to their unique properties. According to a conference in Vienna held in 19871, Psilocybin mushrooms have been eliminated from Schedule A category of drugs. These mushrooms have drug-like properties as well as they leave hallucinogenic effects on the human mind and body. They are sold in dried form or in the form of powder in many regions. The powder form of these mushrooms seems like a drug.

Some professionals also extract Psilocybin compound from mushrooms and sell that compound in crystallized or powdered form. Such buying and selling are done in the black market because the selling and buying of this compound is totally banned because it is a real drug. The use of natural Psilocybin mushrooms, in low or high doses, cannot be restricted totally. It is because naturally grown psilocybin mushrooms cannot be stopped to grow. Nature doesn't allow people to become a drug addict, so there is some legal purpose behind the use of Psilocybin mushrooms. The different forms in which these psilocybin mushrooms are sold are:

- In the form of capsules

- In the form of micro pills
- In the form of powder
- In the form of solid dried mushrooms
- In the form of extracted psilocybin

These mushrooms are sold mostly in the black market in the above-mentioned forms. Fresh mushrooms can be picked up easily, but most of the people are not sure if they are picking up Psilocybin mushrooms (liberty caps etc.), or they are just picking the death caps.

Use of Psilocybin mushrooms should be safe; therefore, you must take care while using these mushrooms. If you are using Psilocybin mushrooms or their capsules, you must not be alone, so if you fall, someone is here to pick you up. The small amount and doses of Psilocybin mushrooms can help you to get rid of negative thoughts and reduce anxiety slowly.

Short Summary

Studies showed that Psilocybin mushrooms themselves are not bad, rather how they are used is good or bad. If someone is using Psilocybin mushrooms for study or research purpose, there is no problem. But if someone is using mushrooms as an alternate drug, or getting relief from stress, in large amounts, it is illegal to use. Many countries of the world have announced Psilocybin mushrooms illegal due to the presence of this Psilocybin compound. The countries where the cultivation and growth of these psilocybin mushrooms are allowed, also have some restrictions and insecurities about them. Some countries have understood that Psilocybin itself is dangerous in large amounts, but the positive use of Psilocybin mushrooms can bring improvement in human thoughts. High dose of everything is bad for health, the same in the case of Psilocybin. The fewer amounts can be useful, but the high dose is always dangerous. Cities like Vancouver has now opened the doors of research on Psilocybin mushrooms due to its unlimited effects on mental health.

CHAPTER SEVEN

Future Aspect of research on Psilocybin mushrooms

The history of Psilocybin mushrooms showed that these mushrooms have big roles to play in the past. The mystics used them, religious personals used them, the drug dealers used them, the healers used them and got their targets successfully. The frequent use of these hallucinogenic mushrooms urged the farmers to cultivate them. But then, Psilocybin discovered, a compound which is responsible for hallucinogenic properties but then considered as a drug. When people started misusing them, governments put bans on these mushrooms. Cultivation became illegal, but still, there are many regions where farmers grow psilocybin mushrooms in their fields and then sell them. Everything depends on intentions if intentions are good, nothing is illegal, but if intentions are bad, everything is illegal.

Scientists, researchers and mycologists are still doing research to find more about Psilocybin mushrooms. They have such properties which can alter the human mind and can put amazing effects on it. Researchers are trying to get such results which can be useful for people with mental disorders. Psilocybin mushrooms have a direct concern with the brain because they activate the neurotransmitters, boosts up the thinking ability after giving first hallucinogenic jerk.

Researches on the Role of Psilocybin Mushrooms

Recent research on Psilocybin mushrooms stated that Psilocybin could help to reduce the depression and its symptoms without putting any side effects like antidepressants. In the people with depression and anxiety problem, the ability to give sudden face expressions is disturbed. They cannot give an immediate reaction and emotional prompt like facial expressions. Their brain is mostly sensitive to negative thing except for positive ones. There are many antidepressant drugs which try to lower the symptoms of depression for depression patients and try to process their emotions. These antidepressants try to turn the button off the negative thoughts and sensitivities and boost positive thinking.

In 2018, small research was done at the Imperial College London, which revealed that the magic mushrooms, which are also known as Psychedelics, play an important role to treat depression. They revive the brain's positive memory and try to reconnect the patient's positive emotions. The compound present in Psilocybin mushrooms, "Psilocybin" reduces the depression, by resetting the memory and activity of the brain.

Depression Treatment

Another research published in the Journal of Neuropharmacology in 2018 by the psychedelic Research group at the Imperial College London. They studied the ability of the Psilocybin drug to affect brain activity related to emotion processing. The results of this research revealed that the patients having depression, responded to Psilocybin. These patients were not responding to any other treatment, and there were no improvements observed in patients, facing other treatments of depression. The use of Psilocybin can avoid the side effects which are faced by patients due to some other antidepressants like "Prozac", which work as the "serotonin reuptake inhibitors" which have been the most commonly used antidepressants.

Leor Roseman is the head of this research, and he said that:

“Our findings are important as they reveal biological changes after psilocybin therapy and, more specifically, they suggest that increased emotional processing is crucial for the treatment to work".

Altering the Brain Activity

The research on using these mushrooms for brain activity was done by the same group in 2018, and the trial was done in a lab. The trial was done on 20 patients, and they all knew that they are under research. These 20 volunteers had chronic depression, and the researchers asked them to stop antidepressants for two weeks. After that, their trial started, and they were given controlled doses of Psilocybin with some psychiatric support. After the first dose, the second dose was given after a week. During the treatment, the patients with depression were passed through fMRI in which they were shown the human faces with different expressions like happy, neutral, scared etc., and the responses of Patients towards those faces were recorded. The changes in the flow of different parts of the brain were also recorded. For these recording, 19 volunteers out of 20 were taken, and their fMRI was recorded. Patients, even during the treatment, said that they are feeling light and they were showing positive expressions towards the faces showed in fMRI. The positive results were received as the patients were showing strong responses towards the emotional faces.

These findings were interesting, and patients went to their homes happily. But researchers wanted to confirm the results that if these positive results are due to Psilocybin mushrooms or not. So, large scale trials were started by the Psychedelic group.

In the large-scale trials, the patients were unaware of the treatment method, and they didn't know that they are receiving the doses of Psilocybin mushrooms. They were confused between SSRI, Placebo and Psilocybin. The purpose of this study was also to observe how long the impact of Psilocybin remains on the brain. They again received positive results. Roseman intends to further investigate the role of Psilocybin in brain activity as he said that,

"We also want to investigate how the amygdala responds a longer time after treatment, which will inform us about longer-term effects – compared to the current study, which was only looked at one day after the therapy."

The unique and different effects

Another paper of Roseman was published in the Journal Frontiers in Pharmacology, in 2018. The team Roseman made a questionnaire and distributed it among the patients to record their experiences, while under the treatment of Psilocybin. The researchers were actually looking for the "mystical experience" which they have studied in the past history. They asked the patients if they felt like they lost the boundaries of themselves, or felt out of time and space. The responses of patients revealed that the stronger the their mystical experience, the less time they took to recover from depression.

The Team Roseman has future plans to conduct research on these mystical feelings, especially. They observed that these mystical feelings have a role to play in reducing the depression of patients.

Recent Researches

A research was done by Sydney Berry in 2018 in which he explained the usage and benefits of Psilocybin mushrooms in detail. He said that now many countries have started to prefer the medicinal use of Psilocybin mushrooms over their negative uses and now they are not strict about the illegality of Psilocybin mushrooms. The psychedelics have the ability to give eye-opening experience to people, and also put the terrifying impacts on people who try to take high doses of these mushrooms.

The city of Vancouver has opened the use of Psilocybin mushrooms for research purpose. The ban is no more considerable. This action was taken due to the results of different researches on these mushrooms. An article in the Canadian Medical Association Journal explained multiple benefits of Psilocybin mushrooms as Psychedelics on mental and physical health. These mushrooms have the ability to bring changes in mood and perception. People start thinking positive after taking these mushrooms. People who have depression problem but they are resistant to antidepressants, have been treated by Psilocybin mushrooms. Those patients got rid of depression in just 3 months, according to a research by Carhart Harris.

People with anxiety problems due to cancer problem can also be treated by Psilocybin mushrooms. The fear of death in such patients can be reduced by Psilocybin treatment. People with chronic migraine can also be treated with the help of these mushrooms. These psilocybin mushrooms are also useful in reducing the chances of depression as well as reducing the psychological diseases. Another positive and interesting research on Psilocybin mushrooms is that it can help to keep the insects away. When any insect tries to come near the place where any form of Psilocybin mushrooms is present, it changes its path. Insects also feel something different in their mind, maybe the compound psilocybin alter the insect mind and urge the insect to eat something other.

CHAPTER EIGHT

Some Popular Psilocybin Mushrooms of the World

Many regions of the world are rich in Psilocybin mushrooms. These mushrooms grow naturally, so no one can put a ban on their natural growth. The countries that have restricted the cultivation of Psilocybin mushrooms due to several reasons cannot restrict the natural growth of these mushrooms in marshlands, gardens and other suitable places. So, mycologists, mushrooms lovers and researchers in addition with mystics, always search for Psilocybin mushrooms, identify them and patent them. Every year, they discover a new species of Psilocybin mushrooms and patent it with the name of discover. Let's discuss some popular Psilocybin Mushrooms and their genera.

The Genus Panaeolus

The genus Panaeolus also comes under Psilocybin mushrooms. Some popular species of this genera are:

Panaeolus Africanus

The *Panaeolus Africanus* belongs to the genus Panaeolus and has a conic cap with convex and hemispheric shape. Its surface is smooth but may have cracks or scales above the cap, these cracks and scales show up when these mushrooms are exposed to the sun. They are viscid when wet, mostly when they are young. The color of these psilocybin mushrooms is grayish, creamy white mostly but sometimes they have reddish-brown color but become grayish with age. Like all Psilocybin mushrooms, these mushrooms also have gills which are attached inside the cap, widely spaced but with an irregular arrangement. They look grayish at first look and become black with age, especially when they produce spores. They stem of these psilocybin mushrooms is 30-50 mm by 4-6 mm thick, firm, protruded towards the apex and equal. The color of the stem is mostly white to pinkish tones; the color of the stem is lighter than its cap.

These mushrooms are mostly found in the region of central Africa and in some regions of Sudan. During the rainy seasons, the mushrooms are found even on elephant dung in these regions. As discussed earlier, these mushrooms also contain Psilocybin and Psilocin; therefore, these mushrooms are Psilocybin mushrooms.

Panaeolus Castaneifolius

Panaeolus castaneifolius which is also known as Murrill regionally is a native Psilocybin mushroom of North and South

American Countries. These mushrooms have a spherical cap which becomes convex with age, curved margins at an early age and then starts to straight with age. The color of this species of mushrooms is smoky gray when they are slightly moist and when they start to dry, the color becomes straw yellow or pale. They are reddish-brown at the edges and margins. They are also gilled mushrooms, and their gills are attached to the inside face and wrinkled to some extent. The color of gills become purplish, gray-black when spores start to mature. The stem of these mushrooms is long and this but narrow at the base. It is gray in color, hollow and tubular. They are identified by their dark, purplish, gray black gills which are gray-black due to their spore's maturity.

They are widely distributed as mentioned before. The South and North American region are rich in this species of Psilocybin mushrooms as discovered by the researchers. They specifically grow in dark places.

Panaeolus Papilionaceous

The cap of this *Panaeolus papilionaceus* is conic in shape which becomes campanulate with age, the margins of its cap have a tooth-like structure in white color. In young fruiting bodies of these mushrooms, the surface of their caps is smooth but horizontally wrinkled having light-colored flesh. The flesh is thick on the underside of the gills. The gills are also attached inside the cap, which is broad to some extent and grayish in color. The grayish black color or gills is mostly unbalanced ripening of spores. The stem of these mushrooms is about 60 to 140 mm long and 1.5 to 3.5 mm thick. It is equally distributed, tubular, fibrous and protruding towards the apex slightly. The mix of brownish and grayish color makes these mushrooms differentiable from other mushrooms.

The whitish tooth-like structures look like a veil of these mushrooms. These mushrooms mostly grow in dung and in the season of fall or spring. They are native to North American and temperate regions of the world. Researchers noticed that these mushrooms look common during the autumn season. These mushrooms also resemble with some other mushrooms like *Panaoelus retirugis* etc. due to the whitish, tooth-like structures. Researchers have found that these mushrooms are identified by the presence of wrinkled cap.

Panaelus Semiovatus

Panaelus semiovatus is a psilocybin mushroom species with conic cap expanding near the convex. The young fruiting bodies are pink in color but become whitish with age. The smooth and wrinkled surface of its cap is due to the environment in which they grow. Whitish gills are attached downside of the cap, but they become brownish in color and then blackish when spores start ripening. They are mostly found in South America and Temperate zones of Europe. According to some studies, this species of psilocybin mushrooms is considered to be non-active for years. It mostly grows on dung. So, researchers looking for this species of mushrooms, mostly look in dung to find these species. It is identified by its viscid cap and large size of its cap as compared to other species.

The other popular species of Psilocybin mushrooms categorized under the genus Panaeolus are:

- Panaeolus antillarum
- Panaeolus cambodginiensis
- Panaeolus castaneifolius
- Panaeolus cyanescens
- Panaeolus fimicola
- Panaeolus foenisecii
- Panaeolus papilionaceus
- Panaeolus subbalteatus
- Panaeolus tropicalis

The Genus Psilocybe

Psilocybe is the most popular genera of Psilocybin mushrooms. They are also mostly called "Psilocybes." Like other mushrooms they are also saprotrophic and get their food from other organisms, they grow mostly in moist places, and their habitat is decaying wood debris, dung, grasslands, mosses etc. All the psilocybes contain Psilocin and Psilocybin compounds which separate the psilocybin mushrooms from other families of Mushrooms. They are identified by their brownish gills with white edges. Good expertise is highly recommended to identify the Psilocybin mushrooms. Some popular species which comes under the category of Psilocybes are:

Psilocybe Aeruginosa

The cap these *Psilocybe Aeroginosa* is convex to campanulate. The cap starts to expand as convex with the passage of time. It shows the shape like low, broad umbo. It is mostly bluish-green at the start, but the color fades away with age. The surface of the cap is mostly viscid due to moisture and humidity. It has margins covered with veil-like flecks. The gills of these mushrooms are brown in color, mostly clay brown, sometimes show a shade of purple and white edges. The stem is thick but swelled at the base. The surface of the stem is covered by white-colored patches. These mushrooms are mostly found in the regions like the British Isles, northern Europe, and in western North America. The perfect habitat for these mushrooms is wood debris, gardens, parks, grassy area at the edges of woodlands, etc. In the region of Pacific Northwest, the Psilocybe aeruginosa grows under the conifers while in Southern California, these mushrooms are found growing under the oak trees. Historically, these mushrooms are reported as poisonous due to enough content of Psilocybin.

Psilocybe atrobrunnea

Psilocybe atrobrunnea is the species of genus Psilocybe which has conic caps, but bluntly conic caps. They have sharp nipple above the cap and are convex with age. The caps of these mushrooms are mostly reddish-brown or blackish reddish brown.

When they get dry, their color converts to pale reddish-brown. The cap has a smooth surface, but viscid when they are moist. These mushrooms also have whitish veil-like structures. The color of gills of these mushrooms is dark purplish-brown and has whitish edges. They have a thick stem with a swelled base and equally distributed. The spores of these mushrooms are violaceous, dark brown in color and become black with the passage of time.

These mushrooms are usually found near sphagnum bogs, growing under conifers, woodlands and their fruiting start in September and October mostly. This species of Psilocybin mushrooms is found in Michigan, upper New York regions of United States. They are also reported from British Columbia and central to northern Europe (including Great Britain, Czech Republic, Slovakia, Finland, France, Germany, Sweden and Poland). It shows that these mushrooms are widely distributed. This species also has resemblance with some other Psilocybe species.

Psilocybe Aucklandii

The cap of *Psilocybe aucklandii* is conical in shape when they are immature and starts becoming plane with maturity. The margins of this species are striate and split with the passage of time. This species has no veil-like structures. The color of its cap is dark brown, but when it dries, the color becomes pale yellow or straw brown. It is discussed earlier that most Psilocybin mushrooms show bruises and become bluish when injured, same is the case with Psilocybe aucklandii. They show bruises and start to show a blue color when they are injured. The gills of these mushrooms are attached under the cap and are grayish-yellow in color and become darker with maturity. The thick stem of these mushrooms is covered with silky white fibrils, have brownish flesh and bluish bruising. The spores are purple colored and are distributed and scattered by different means. Psilocybe aucklandii are distributed naturally, and they like to grow on the soil rich with wood debris.

The name Aucklandii belongs to the Auckland city New Zealand. They are only found around the New Zealand, near the pines and woodlands. During the transport of woods, trees etc., these species have high chances to transfer to other temperate zones of the world.

Psilocybe Mexicana

This species of mushrooms is one of the most popular species. It is the one which was used by old mystics and was a part of religious rituals in ancient times. The cap of this strange species of mushrooms is conical to campanulate and becomes convex at maturity. The margins of its cap have fine fibrils, and its color is brown to deep orange which fades away on drying and become yellowish. The gills are attached inside the cap which is pale gray to dark purplish-brown on maturity, and edges become whitish. The stem of *Psilocybe mexicana* is thick and long with straw yellow to brownish color and becomes darker with age or any injury. The region of Mexico is rich in *Psilocybe mexicana,* and it mostly grows in horse pastures, soils rich with manure and fields.

The first research on Psilocybin mushrooms was started by *Psilocybe Mexicana.* Mystics and healers were using this mushroom, but they didn't know about their name and exact properties. This psilocybin mushroom was also worshipped by old people as they believed that this is a powerful mushroom. They think that this mushroom has some powers from God.

Psilocybe Cubensis

Another most popular Psilocybin mushroom from Psilocybe genera is "*Psilocybe cubensis*". It is one of the most commonly available psychedelics. There are some other names of this Psilocybe including *Stropharia cubensis, Stropharia cyanescens and Stropharia caerulescens.* It is also known as "Mexican mushroom" and magic mushroom or shroom. As compared to other mushrooms, this mushroom is easy to grow. But thanks to nature, this magical mushroom grows naturally most of the times. It also contains Psilocin and Psilocybin which are responsible for many of its medicinal, and hallucinogenic properties. Like *Psilocybe mexicana,* it is also the psilocybin mushroom which played an important part in research on Psilocybin mushrooms. It is also known as golden tops because of its golden colored cap.

The cap of *Psilocybe cubensis* is conic and campanulate, which becomes convex at the edges. Gills are attached downside the cap and are grayish brown in color which become purplish-black with age. The stem is thick and whitish but bruising may appear even due to minor injuries. This species of mushrooms is found in the southeastern region of United States, Mexico, Cuba, Central America, northern South America, in the subtropical Far East (India, Thailand, Vietnam and Cambodia), also in the regions of Australia. It is mostly seen in two months of its fruiting like in May and June.

Some Other Important Psilocybin Mushrooms and Their Genera

The most well-known genera of Psilocybin mushrooms are:

- Panaeolus
- Psilocybe
- Conocybe
- Gymnopilus
- Inocybe
- Pluteus

Summary and conclusion

Fungi are a separate kingdom due to its diversity and number of species. It is a separate kingdom because it has different characteristics than both animals and plants. They mostly look like plants, but they are dependent on other organisms for their food. The food of fungi is other plants, animal debris, dung, rotten plants, and corpses of animals. They gain their organic food and fulfil their nutritional requirements from other organisms. They used to grow in humid places and in wet environments mostly. Whenever their spores find suitable conditions, they start to grow. Mushrooms are the fruiting bodies of fungus. It is a very diverse group of fungus with thousands of species and different types. Some are edible fungus, others are poisonous, and some are hallucinogenic. Hallucinogenic mushrooms are very unique mushrooms in properties; therefore, they are also called "Magic mushrooms." There is a specific compound present in these mushrooms, which are responsible for its hallucinogenic characteristics, the Psilocybin; therefore, these mushrooms are also called Psilocybin mushrooms.

Researchers found fungus growing in caves around Paris, whose history dates back in the 1600s when French gardeners found that the humid and cool environment of caves is suitable for mushroom cultivation. Therefore mushrooms were cultivated at large scale in caves. In Netherlands, mushrooms were introduced for cultivation in the 1800s but on small scales. Then after some time, large scale cultivation of mushrooms was done in marl mines in Limburg. After caves and mines, other methods of mushroom cultivation were developed, which then resulted in high mushroom yields in the region. Before that, mushrooms were specific, and they were only available for elites. Dutch people had the strictest rules for mushroom cultivation, and they had their own specific controls over the cultivation. That was the reason that the Netherlands became the largest mushroom producing country 50 years ago. But then, China and the USA came into the competition of mushroom cultivation. China produces about 70% of the world's mushrooms now. So, China is in the first position in mushroom cultivation, and then comes the USA and Netherlands.

Psilocybin mushroom pictures, discovered from the ruin of Mayan temple. History shows that the Aztec people had too much belief on a specific Psilocybin mushroom (Psilocybe mexicana) that they name it Teonanacatl, which means "God's Flesh." A Franciscan in the 16th century went on an expedition with a team and reported about the beliefs of Aztec about "God's Flesh," but misguided Catholics. Catholics were running a campaign against Paganism at that time, and they were misguided about the usage of mushrooms. They restrict the use of Psilocybin mushrooms as they thought that Pagans worship these mushrooms. This all resulted in the planned demise of this culture, but they couldn't destroy some evidence. The research and reports by Franciscan Bernardino De Sahagun are the ultimate source of knowledge about usage of Psilocybin mushrooms by Aztec tribes.

Psilocybin mushrooms are also known as magic mushrooms as well as hallucinogenic mushrooms, which cover some part of the earth. These mushrooms have a great history like they have been used in religious rituals as well as in the holy meals. The old mystics and healers used these mushrooms in their programs without knowing their actual name and their content. The content of Psilocybin mushrooms remained hidden for centuries, and people blindly used them as part of their lives. Many people in the past used these mushrooms to treat their mental and physical health. The history of Psilocybin mushrooms is too long that it needs a whole separate book to explain. Researchers who were interested in studying mushrooms and different species of mushrooms found the backward areas of the world worshipping these psilocybin mushrooms. They tried to find the reasons why people used to worship Psilocybin mushrooms. They also found the sketches and carvings of these mushrooms in caves and old found plates. It was then assumed that ancient people used Psilocybin mushrooms for different purposes. Ancient people found the psilocybin mushrooms powerful; therefore, they started to think that these mushrooms have godly powers. It was the habit of ancient people that whenever they found something more powerful, they made their sculptures and accepted them as their gods. Obviously, that was a wrong behavior, but that was due to less exposure and lack of education. These mushrooms are found in many regions of the world including America, Australia, Canada, UK, Mexico, Asia, Africa, in short, only Antarctica is a place where there is no chance of presence of these mushrooms. Otherwise, they can be found anywhere they have a compatible environment. Mexico is a country from where the research on these mushrooms started first, and then it continued to Paris and so on. The reason behind is, in Mexico, the old mystics and healers had the habit of using specific mushrooms for their performances, but they didn't know the names. The religious meetings and holy meals were not completed without these magic mushrooms. Researchers found the mushrooms and found them interesting; therefore, they started their research.

Then time changed, and science improved. People got educated, and they started to control the powers of these mushrooms for their own purposes. The hallucinogenic properties of these mushrooms attracted common people and researchers to get benefits. Many people tried t eat them and got nausea and other problems; therefore, people are advised not to eat mushrooms without identification. After the discovery of the benefits of Psilocybin mushrooms and their amazing properties, their demand increased. So the trials of their cultivation started. Common people tried to cultivate these mushrooms for their own purposes while the researchers and scientists started trials for the cultivation of these mushrooms in their laboratories. They wanted to grow the cultures of Psilocybin mushrooms in labs to study them more and to explore more about psilocybin mushrooms. Scientists got success in growing the cultures of Psilocybin mushrooms in laboratories. They also talked about different mediums on which we can grow the cultures of Psilocybin mushrooms. The successful cultures of Psilocybin mushrooms can be used for field trials and cultivation.

The in-depth studies revealed that there are two major compounds in Psilocybin mushrooms, which are responsible for the unique properties of these mushrooms. These two compounds are Psilocybin and Psilocin. These compounds are found naturally in mushrooms, but the studies also revealed that they were not present in these mushrooms thousands of years ago. The mushrooms got the genes of these compounds through horizontal gene transfer. The horizontal gene transfer was responsible for making these mushrooms as Psilocybin mushrooms and hallucinogenic mushrooms. Psilocybin is a crystalline compound with white crystals that cannot be dissolved in simple water. The chemical and physical properties of Psilocybin mushrooms depend upon the chemical and physical properties of Psilocybin and Psilocin. Psilocin is the degrading product of Psilocybin. The precursor of both of these compounds is Tryptophan, which reveals that these compounds have an amino acid origin. Psilocybin is not found separate mostly; therefore, it is extracted from Psilocybin mushrooms.

This compound has been categorized under the name of A-class drug due to its hallucinogenic and drug-like properties. When the drug-like properties of these mushrooms revealed, many countries put a ban on the cultivation of these mushrooms. Now, Psilocybin mushrooms are illegal in many regions of the world. The buying, selling, and cultivation of these mushrooms are not legal in many countries. The reason behind these restrictions is the misuse of Psilocybin mushrooms. Many people started taking high doses of Psilocybin mushrooms, which made them drug addicts. But scientists and researchers think differently: they try to explore Psilocybin mushrooms due to their unique characteristics. The legality and illegality of Psilocybin mushrooms are different in many countries. Some countries allow the buying and selling of spores of Psilocybin mushrooms but don't allow their cultivation. Some countries allow the buying, selling, and cultivation of magic mushrooms (a developmental stage in Psilocybin mushrooms). But in some countries the buying, selling and cultivation of Psilocybin mushrooms in any form is illegal. In some countries, if anyone is found with psilocybin mushrooms, he is punished and also sent to the drug rehabilitation centers forcefully.

There are mainly six genera of Psilocybin mushrooms, including Panaeolus, Psilocybe, Conocybe, Gymnopilus, Inocybe, and Pluteus. All these six genera are further divided into several species. There are thousands of species in all these general. Different regions of the world are rich in these species. The regions of North and South America are rich in Psilocybe and

Panaeolus genus. *Psilocybe cubensis* and *Psilocybe Mexicana* are two main species of genus Psilocybe which are most popular species.

Studies showed that Psilocybin mushrooms are useful in the treatment of many mental disorders. They can really help to reduce the symptoms of chronic depression and anxiety. Many psychological and mental disorders can be treated with these mushrooms; therefore, they are also called "psychedelics." They have ability to bring changes in mind and put positive effects on mind, but one should care about the doses. High doses of Psilocybin mushrooms can be dangerous and can lead to death therefore one should not use psilocybin mushrooms without proper consultation and without any supervision. Research also revealed that microdoses of Psilocybin mushrooms could convert negative thoughts into positive thoughts. Although a little dose of psilocybin causes nausea, hallucinations, etc. but it doesn't cause sleepiness. One may feel that he is not in this world; he is in another world where there is no stress and no work to do. Due to such feelings, researchers say that these mushrooms can free someone from chronic depression because of its compound Psilocybin. Psilocybin mushrooms are also sold in the dried form as well as powder and capsules. A lot of research is in the tunnel to explore more about these unique magic mushrooms and to know more about its magical properties.

Conclusion

The in-depth study on these psilocybin mushrooms reveals that actually, there is nothing wrong with the Psilocybin mushrooms. The wrong is with people who use them for negative purposes. Psilocybin mushrooms grow naturally, and they have psilocybin naturally in them. It means that it is a gift of nature, but we have to explore more and learn more about their benefits. There is nothing useless created by nature, and everything has a positive role to play, the same is the case of psilocybin mushrooms. If some people consider them as drug, there are some people who use to worship them due to the powers of these mushrooms.

The legality and illegality of psilocybin mushrooms should not be a hurdle in research because there is no restriction or ban on research. If there are good intentions behind the use of psilocybin mushrooms, the use is not considered illegal. They are illegal only when they are used for negative purposes. The mafia has used Psilocybin mushrooms for their purposes and throws many people into drug abuse. But now science has discovered such compounds that can mimic the effects of psilocybin mushrooms. If all people understand the positive use of Psilocybin mushrooms, they can also enjoy the benefits of these magic mushrooms. A little more research is needed to make these mushrooms as antidepressants. They can be a great replacement for antidepressants because they have no hidden side effects.

Some Species of Psilocybin mushrooms

There are thousands of species of Psilocybin mushrooms. Few of those mushrooms are:

- *Copelandia anomala*
- *Copelandia bispola*
- *Copelandia chlorocystis*
- *Copelandia tropicalis*
- *Copelandia lentisporus*
- *Copelandia westii*
- *Inocye corydalina*
- *Inocybe tricolor*
- *Inocybe haemacta*
- *Inocybe aeruginascens*
- *Panaeolus bisporus*
- *Panaeolus africanus*
- *Panaeolus affinis*
- *Panaeolus chlorocystis*
- *Panaeolus lentisporus*
- *Panaeolus microsporus*
- *Panaeolus fimicola*
- *Panaeolus cambodginiensis*
- *Conocybe cyanopus*
- *Conocybe siligineoides*
- *Conocybe kuehneiriana*

- *Gymnopilus junonius*
- *Gymnopilus braendlei*
- *Gymnopilus luteus*
- *Gymnopilus purpuratus*
- *Gymnopilus intermedius*
- *Pluteus glaucus*
- *Pluteus nigroviridis*
- *Pluteus villosus*
- *Pluteus brunneidiscus*
- *Pluteus phaeocyanopus*
- *Pluteus cyanopus*
- *Psilocybe angustipleurocystidiata*
- *Psilocybe antioquiensis Guzmán*
- *Psilocybe aquamarina*
- *Psilocybe araucariicola*
- *Psilocybe armandii Guzmán*

Appendices

Species of Psychedelic Mushrooms:

Some important species of psychedelic mushrooms with their accepted genera and specie name are as follows:

Genus Copelandia:

- Copelandia anomala
- Copelandia bispola
- Copelandia chlorocystis
- Copelandia tropicalis
- Copelandia lentisporus
- Copelandia westii

Genus Inocybe:

- Inocye corydalina
- Inocybe tricolor

- Inocybe haemacta
- Inocybe aeruginascens

Genus Panaeolus:

- Panaeolus bisporus
- Panaeolus africanus
- Panaeolus affinis
- Panaeolus chlorocystis
- Panaeolus lentisporus
- Panaeolus microsporus
- Panaeolus fimicola
- Panaeolus cambodginiensis

Genus Conocybe:

- Conocybe cyanopus
- Conocybe siligineoides
- Conocybe kuehneiriana

Genus Gymnopilus:

- Gymnopilus junonius

- Gymnopilus braendlei
- Gymnopilus luteus
- Gymnopilus purpuratus
- Gymnopilus intermedius

Two additional studies using psilocybin have been completed: one at New York University (NYU) Langone Medical Center in New York City and one at Johns Hopkins Medical School in Baltimore. They used trained monitors with patients for both studies as they experienced the effects of the drug, which can lead to hallucinations.

In the NYU study, 29 patients with advanced cancer were given either a single dose of psilocybin or the B vitamin known as niacin, both in conjunction with psychotherapy. After seven weeks, the patients switched treatments (a cross-over study). In 60% to 80% of the patients receiving psilocybin, relief from distress occurred rapidly and lasted over six months. The long-term effect was evaluated by researchers looking at test scores for depression and anxiety.

In the Johns Hopkins study, researchers treated 51 adults with advanced cancer with a small dose of psilocybin followed five weeks later with a higher dose, with a 6-month follow-up. As with the NYU study, about 80% of participants experienced clinically significant relief from their anxiety and depression that lasted up to six months.

Studies showed that patients those used magic mushrooms have no regrets and feel their world is a better place because of magic mushrooms.

Genera	**Species**	**Example**
Copelandia	Few	*Panaeolus cambodginiensis*
Gymnopilus	200	*Gymnopilus cyanopalmicola*
Inocybe	1400	*Inocybe aeruginascens*
Mycena	500 above	*Mycena cyanorrhiza*
Panaeolus	98	*Panaeolus cyanescens*
Pholiotina	100 above	*Pholiota gummosa*
Pluteus	300	*Pluteus brunneidiscus*
Psilocybe	500 above	*Psilocybe cubensis*

Sexual reproduction is the recombination of the genetic material from two parent individuals to form a new one. The container of genetic material donated by each parent is known as a gamete. The gametes of fungi are called spores. A spore is a compact, protected cell, capable of remaining alive but dormant for long periods of time until it finds a suitable home. All of the fungi we will discuss in this book are known as Basidiomycetes, since they produce their spores on basidia, tiny baseball-bat-shaped protuberances lining their gills, the blade-like structures arranged in a radial pattern on the underside of the cap, or pileus.7 The pileus is held aloft on the end of a cylindrical stem, known to mycologists as a stipe.

Spore Discharge

Let's return to our cow patty and its lonely mushroom. Zoom in closer: deep in shadow, millions of microscopic, baseball-bat-shaped basidia stick out from the flat faces of the gills lining the underside of the parasol, and at the wide end of each basidium stand four ovoid, purple-black spores. Each spore is perched like a top upon a tiny horn-shaped protuberance at the outer end of the basidium, known as a sterignta. The air around the gills is moist and much cooler than that around the mushroom, thanks to the wonders of evaporative cooling taking place on the sun-beaten upper face of the cap. As the air cools, water condenses around the spore and its tiny stand, and a droplet begins to form at the place they join. The droplet grows until it can no longer support its own structure, its surface tension breaks, and the water from the droplet spreads out over the body of the spore. The force of this action draws the spore toward the sterigma. The Biology of Mushrooms I 11 steligma, being somewhat elastic, collapses slightly beneath the weight of the spore, only to push back with an equal and opposite force and catapult the spore from its perch into the open space beyond the face of the gills. The amount of force is precisely calculated to hurtle the spore far enough to clear the surface of its own gill, but not so far that it smacks into the facing one. Instead, it succumbs to gravity and is pulled straight down and out below the bottom face of the mushroom, where with a little luck, it will be carried away by a gust of wind, along with millions of its siblings. When the wind in our field subsides, two spores from our mushroom have settled onto a patch of grass, where an electron scanning micrograph of Psilocybe cubensis they now wait patiently for something or someone to bring them closer together. Fungal Growth Now picture a cow, maybe the one who made that same cow patty from the beginning of the chapter. The cow is munching on the grass in our field because that's what cows like to do, and sooner or later, she eats the blades of grass upon which sit our lonely spores, munching them down with her lunch. Swallowed whole with the grass, they are swept through her digestive tract only to emerge some time later at the other end. Fortunately, the spores are resilient and well armored and suffer no ill effects from their wild ride through the cow's guts. Better than that, for their troubles, they find themselves smack in the middle of a pile of their favorite food: cow shit. Soon afterward, each of our spores germinates, its cells dividing and slowly growing out into the delectable and nutrient-rich materials in the cow patty.

Growing fungi consist of networks of hyphae: tubular, filamentous cells that expand and divide at their forward tips, occasionally branching to create fork- or tan-like structures. Masses of hyphae are known collectively as the mycelium of the fungus. To the naked eye, fungal mycelium often appears as white, fuzzy, or hair-like growth on the surface of the food source (or substrate), such as you might see on the underside of an upturned log. Most fungi spend the majority of their days as an undifferentiated mycelium, only occasionally forming specialized, complex structures such as mushrooms. Hyphal growth is also invasive, meaning it occurs within and often throughout the substrate. Digestive enzymes secreted from the tips of the advancing mycelium into their surroundings, degrade the substrate into simpler organic molecules, to be absorbed or engulfed by the mycelium as it marches along. In effect, fungi do their digesting on the outside. While we tend to process our meals in the privacy of our own insides, fungi prefer to eat out. All of the fungi we discuss in this book are saprophytes or saprobes, meaning that they derive their nutrition from non-living organic matter, in this case, dead or decaying plants. This is in contrast to parasitic fungi, which colonize and digest living organisms, often killing their host at the end, and mycorrhizal fungi, which live in a symbiotic relationship with their plant hosts.

Psilocybin Mushrooms with names of their discoverers

Psilocybe
Psilocybe acadiensis (Smith) Psilocybe acutipilea (Speg.) Guzmán, psychoactive Psilocybe aerugineomaculans (Hohn.) Singer & A.H. Smith Psilocybe allenii Borov., Rockefeller & P.G.Werner Psilocybe alutacea Y.S. Chang & A.K. Mills Psilocybe angustipleurocystidiata Guzmán, psychoactive

Psilocybe antioquiensis Guzmán, Saldarr., Pineda, G. Garcia & L.-F. Velazquez, psychoactive

Psilocybe atlantis Guzmán, Hanlin & C. White, psychoactive

Psilocybe aquamarina (Pegler) Guzmán

Psilocybe araucariicola P. S. Silva, likely psychoactive[1]

Psilocybe armandii Guzmán & S.H. Pollock, psychoactive

Psilocybe aucklandii Guzmán, C.C. King & Bandala, psychoactive

Psilocybe aztecorum R. Heim

Psilocybe aztecorum var. bonetii (Guzman) Guzmán (a.k.a. Psilocybe bonetii Guzmán)

Psilocybe azurescens Stamets & Gartz

Psilocybe baeocystis Singer & A.H. Smith

Psilocybe banderillensis Guzmán

Psilocybe bispora Guzman, Franco-Molano and Ramírez-Guillén

Psilocybe brasiliensis Guzmán

Psilocybe brunneocystidiata Guzmán & Horak

Psilocybe cubensis

Psilocybe cabiensis Guzmán, M. Torres & Ram.-Guill[2][3]

Psilocybe caeruleoannulata Singer ex Guzmán

Psilocybe caerulescens

Psilocybe caerulescens Murrill var. caerulescens
Psilocybe caerulescens var. ombrophila (R. Heim) Guzmán
Psilocybe caerulipes (Peck) Sacc.
Psilocybe carbonaria Singer
Psilocybe caribaea Guzmán, T.J. Baroni & Tapia
Psilocybe chiapanensis Guzmán
Psilocybe chuxiongensis T.Ma & K.D.Hyde
Psilocybe cinnamomea J.F.Liang, Yang K.Li & Ye Yuan – China[4]
Psilocybe collybioides Singer & A.H. Smith
Psilocybe columbiana Guzmán
Psilocybe congolensis Guzmán
Psilocybe coprinifacies (Rolland) Pouzar s. auct., non s.Herink, non s. Krieglsteiner (see discussion)
Psilocybe cordispora R. Heim
Psilocybe cubensis (Earle) Singer
Psilocybe cyanescens Wakef. (non sensu Krieglsteiner)
Psilocybe cyanofibrillosa Guzmán & Stamets

Conocybes
Conocybe apala (very common)

Conocybe aurea Conocybe cyanopus (psychoactive) Conocybe elegans Conocybe filaris (deadly) Conocybe kuehneriana (psychoactive)
Conocybe moseri Conocybe reticulata Conocybe rickenii Conocybe siligineoides (psychoactive) Conocybe smithii (psychoactive) Conocybe tenera (type species) Conocybe volviradicata

Inocybes
Inocybe caballeroi C.E.Hermos. & Esteve-Rav. 2005 Inocybe caespitosa Velen. 1922 Inocybe caespitosella Speg. 1926 Inocybe calamistrata (Fr.) Gillet 1876 – Europe Inocybe calamistratoides E.Horak 1978

Inocybe calcaris Métrod 1953

Inocybe calida Velen. 1920 – United Kingdom

Inocybe californica Kauffman 1924

Inocybe calopedes Matheny & Bougher 2010

Inocybe calospora Quél. 1881 – Europe

Inocybe candidipes Kropp & Matheny 2004

Inocybe canescens J.Favre 1955

Inocybe carelica Singer 1938

Inocybe caroticolor – China[5]

Inocybe carpinacea Velen. 1947

Inocybe castanea Peck 1904

Inocybe castaneoides Peck 1913

Inocybe castanopsis Hruby 193

Inocybe casuarinae Corner & E. Horak 1979

Inocybe catalaunica Singer 1947 – United Kingdom

Inocybe caucasica Singer 1937

Inocybe cavipes (Britzelm.) Sacc. & Traverso 1910

Inocybe cerasphora Singer 1953

Inocybe cercocarpi Kropp, Matheny & Hutchison 2013 – USA[3]

Inocybe cerea E. Horak 1978

Inocybe cerina (Malençon) Bon 1996

Inocybe cervicolor (Pers.) Quél. 1886 – Europe

Inocybe chalcodoxantha Grund & D.E.Stuntz 1968

Inocybe chelanensis D.E.Stuntz 1947

Inocybe chilensis Singer 1965

Inocybe chondroderma – Pacific Northwest, North America[6]

Inocybe chondrospora Einhell. & Stangl 1979

Inocybe chrysocephala F.H.Nishida 1988

Inocybe chrysochroa Tak. Kobay. & Courtec. 1993

Inocybe cinchonensis (Murrill) Dennis 1968

Inocybe cincinnata (Fr.) Quél. 1872 – United Kingdom[7]

Inocybe cinerascentipes Huijsman 1955

Inocybe cingulata E.Horak 1979

Inocybe cingulatipes (Corner & E. Horak) Garrido 1988

Inocybe cinnabarina Hruby 1930

Inocybe cinnamomea A.H.Sm. 1941 – Western Cape Province

Inocybe cinnamomicolor Reumaux 2001

Inocybe cistobulbipes Esteve-Rav. & Vila 2002

Inocybe citrinofolia Métrod 1956

Inocybe clavata Takah. Kobay. 2002

Inocybe claviger E.Horak & Bas 1981

Inocybe coelestium Kuyper 1985 (psychoactive)

Inocybe coerulescens Kobayasi 1952

Inocybe collivaga Velen. 1920

Inocybe comatella (Peck) Sacc. 1887

Inocybe concinnula J.Favre 1955

Inocybe confusa P.Karst. 1888

Inocybe congregata A.Pearson 1950 – Western Cape Province

Inocybe conica P.Larsen 1931

Inocybe conicoalba E.Horak 1979

Inocybe connexa Kauffman 1924

Inocybe conspicuispora Buyck & Eyssart. 1999

Mycomorphbox Poison.png Inocybe cookei Bres. 1892 – United Kingdom[4]

Inocybe copriniformis Reumaux 2005

Inocybe corcontica Velen. 1920

Inocybe cordae Velen. 1920

Inocybe corneri (E.Horak) Garrido 1988

Inocybe corrubescens Singer 1931

Inocybe cortinata Rolland 1901

Inocybe corydalina Quél. 1875 (psychoactive) – Europe

Inocybe crassicystidiata Pegler 1983 – Martinique

Inocybe crassipes (Cooke & Massee) Pegler 1965

Inocybe cryptocystis D.E.Stuntz 1954 – United Kingdom

Inocybe curreyi (Berk.) Sacc. 1887 – United Kingdom

Inocybe curvipes P.Karst. 1890 – Africa, Europe

Inocybe cutifracta Petch 1917 - India, Sri Lanka[8]

Inocybe cyaneovirescens Henn. 1900

Inocybe cylindrispora Murrill 1945

Inocybe cylindrocystis G.F.Atk. 1918

Inocybe cystidiosa (A.H.Sm.) Singer 1951

Inocybe davisiana Kauffman 1924

Inocybe deborae E.Ferrari 2003

Inocybe decemgibbosa (Kühner) Vauras 1997 – United Kingdom

Inocybe decipiens Bres. 1892

Inocybe decipientoides Peck 1907

Inocybe deianae Eyssart. 2007

Inocybe deminuta Peck 1906

Inocybe demitrata Velen. 1920

Inocybe dentifera Velen. 1947

Inocybe derbschii Schwöbel & Stangl 1982

Inocybe desquamans Peck 1906

Inocybe destruens E.Horak 1978

Inocybe dewrangia Grgur. 1997

Inocybe diabolica Vauras 1994

Inocybe dilutecinnamomea Singer 195

Inocybe diminuta Peck 1906

Inocybe dissocystis Singer 1953

Inocybe distincta Latha, Manim. & Matheny 2016

Inocybe dolichospora Malençon 1970

Inocybe dulcamara (Pers.) P.Kumm. 1871[7]

Inocybe dulcamaroides Kühner 1988

Inocybe dunensis P.D.Orton 1960 – United Kingdom

Inocybe duriuscula Rea 1908 – United Kingdom

Inocybe earleana Kauffman 1924

Inocybe echinosimilis (E.Horak) Garrido 1988

Inocybe echinospora Egeland 1913

Inocybe egenula J.Favre 1955

Inocybe elegans Reumaux 2001

Inocybe elliptica Takah.Kobay. 2002

Inocybe emergens (Cleland) Grgur. 1997 Inocybe enigmatica Matheny & Aime 2012 Inocybe epidendron Matheny, Aime & T.W.Henkel 2003 Inocybe ericetorum Vauras & Kokkonen 2013[2] Inocybe erinaceomorpha Stangl & J.Veselský 1979 – United Kingdom
Inocybe erubescens A.Blytt 1905 (= I. patouillardii) red-staining inocybe (deadly poisonous) Inocybe erythospilota Grund & D.E.Stuntz 1984 Inocybe erythrobasis Singer 1954 Inocybe eurycystis E.H.L.Krause 1929 Inocybe euthelella Peck 1915 Inocybe eutheloides Peck 1887 Inocybe excoriata Peck 1904 Inocybe exigua (Cleland) Grgur. 1997 Inocybe exilis (Kuyper) Jacobsson & E.Larss. 2008

Gymnopilus
G. baileyi (Berk. & Broome) Pegler (1965) G. bakeri Dennis (1970)

G. bellulus (Peck) Murrill (1917)

G. braendlei (Peck) Hesler (1969)

G. brevipes (Cleland) Grgur. (1997)

G. brittoniae (Murrill) Singer (1975)

G. brunneodiscus (Peck) Murrill (1917)

G. bryophilus Murrill (1913

G. caeruloviresc ens Z.S. Bi (1991)

G. californicus (Earle) Murrill (1912)

G. cantharelloides Camboni & Migl. (2006)

G. capitatus Guzm.-Dáv. & Guzmán (1986)

G. castaneus Murrill

G. chilensis Singer (1969)

G. chrysimyces (Berk.) Manjula (1983)

G. chrysites (Berk.) Singer (1962

G. chrysopellus (Berk. & M.A. Curtis) Murrill (1913)

G. chrysotrichoides Murrill (1943)

G. communis Guzm.-Dáv. (1994)

G. condensus (Peck) Murrill (1917)

G. corsicus Romagn. (1977)

G. corticophilus B.J. Rees (1999)

G. crassitunicatus Guzm.-Dáv. (1998)
G. croceoluteus Hesler (1969)
G. crocias (Berk. & Broome) Singer (1955)
G. crociphyllus (Cooke & Massee) Pegler (1965)
G. crocophyllus (Sacc.) Pegler (1965)
G. cyanopalmicola Guzm.-Dáv. (2006)
G. decipiens (W.G. Sm.) P.D. Orton (1960) G. decoratus Murrill G. decurrens Hesler (1969) G. depressus Murrill (1913) G. dilepis (Berk. & Broome) Singer (1951) G. dryophilus Murrill (1943) G. dulongjiangensis M. Zang (1987) G. earlei Murrill (1913) G. echinulisporus Murrill G. edulis (Peck) Murrill (1917) G. elongatipes Z.S. Bi (1986) G. epileatum Ryvarden (2007) G. eucalyptorum (Cleland) Singer (1947) G. excentriciformis Singer (1969)

G. fagicola Murrill

G. farinaceus Murrill

G. ferruginosus B.J. Rees (2001)

G. fibrillosipes Murrill

G. filiceus (Cooke) Singer (1955)

G. flavidellus Murrill

G. flavifolius Murrill (1946)

G. flavipunctatus (Speg.) Singer (1950)

G. flavus (Bres.) Singer (1951)

G. foedatus (Peck) Murrill (1912)

G. fulgens (J. Favre & Maire) Singer (1951)

G. fulvellus (Peck) Murrill (1912)

G. fulvicolor Murrill (1943)

G. fulviconicus Murrill (1945)

G. fulvosquamulosus Hesler (1969)

G. fuscosquamulosus Hesler (1969)

G. galerinopsis Guzm.-Dáv. (1994)

G. giganteus Natarajan & Raman (1983)

G. granulosus (Peck) Murrill (1917)

G. hainanensis T.H. Li & W.M. Zhang (2001)

G. helvoliceps Berk. & M.A. Curtis

G. hemipenetrans Guzm.-Dáv. (1994)

G. hillii Murrill

G. hispidellus Murrill (1913)

G. humicola Harding ex Singer (1962)

G. hybridus (Gillet) Maire 1933

G. hypholomoides Murrill (1913)

G. igniculus Deneyer, P.-A. Moreau & Wuilb. (2002)

G. imperialis (Speg.) Singer (1951)

G. intermedius (Singer) Singer (1951)

G. jalapensis Murrill

G. janthinosarx (Singer) Singer (1951)

G. josserandii Antonín (2000)

G. junonius (Fr.) P.D. Orton (1960)

G. karnalensis S.M. Kulk. (1990)

G. karrara Grgur. (1997)

G. konkinyerius Grgur. (1997)

G. lacticolor Murrill

G. laricicola J. Favre (1960)

G. lateritius (Pat.) Murrill

G. latus Murrill
G. lepidotus Hesler (1969)
G. levis Raithelh. (1974)
G. liquiritiae (Pers.) P. Karst. (1879)
G. longipes Guzm.-Dáv. & Guzmán (1986)
G. longisporus Murrill
G. ludovicianus Murrill
G. luteocarneus Hesler (1969)
G. luteofolius (Peck) Singer (1951)
G. luteoviridis Thiers (1959)
G. lutescens Hesler (1969)
G. luteus (Peck) Hesler (1969)
G. macrocheilocystidiatus Guzm.-Dáv. & Guzmán (1986)
G. magnificus Guzm.-Dáv. & Guzmán (1986)
G. magnus (Peck) Murrill (1917)
G. marasmioides (Berk.) Singer (1955)
G. marginatus B.J. Rees (1999)
G. maritimus
G. marticorenai Garrido (1988)
G. medius Guzm.-Dáv. (1994)

G. megasporus Grgur. (1997)

G. melleus Hesler (1969)

G. mesosporus E. Horak (1989)

G. microloxus Singer (1977)

G. micromegas (Berk.) Manjula (1983)

G. microsporus (Singer) Singer (1951)

G. minutosporus Natarajan & Raman (1983)

G. mitis Hesler (1969)

G. moabus Grgur. (1997)

G. mullaunius Grgur. (1997)

G. multifolius (Peck) Murrill (1917)

G. nashii Murrill (1913)

G. naucorioides Hesler (1969)

G. nevadensis Guzm.-Dáv. & Guzmán (1991)

G. nitens (Cooke & Massee) Dhanch. (1991)

G. njalaensis (Beeli) Pegler (1966)

G. norfolkensis B.J. Rees & Lepp (2000)

G. noviholocirrhus S. Ito & S. Imai (1940)

G. novoguineensis Hongo (1974)

G. obscurus Hesler (1969)

G. ochraceus Høil. (1998)

G. odini (Fr.) Bon & P. Roux (2002)

G. olivaceobrunneus S.M. Kulk. (1990)

G. ombrophilus Miyauchi (2004)

G. omphalina Murrill

G. oregonensis Murrill

G. ornatulus Murrill

G. oxylepis (Berk. & Broome) Singer (1955)

G. pachycystis Singer (1989)

G. pacificus Hesler (1969)

G. pallidus Murrill

G. palmicola Murrill (1913)

G. panelloides E. Horak & Corner (1989)

G. panurensis (Berk.) Pegler (1988)

G. parrumbalus Grgur. (1997)

G. parvisporus B.J. Rees (1999)

G. parvisquamulosus Hesler (1969)

G. parvulus Murrill (1913)

G. patriae B.J. Rees (1999)

G. peliolepis (Speg.) Singer (1951)

G. penetrans (Fr.) Murrill (1912)
G. perisporius Garrido (1988)
G. permollis Murrill
G. perplexus B.J. Rees (2003)
G. pholiotoides Murrill (1913)
G. piceinus Murrill
G. picreus (Pers.) P. Karst. (1879)
G. pleurocystidiatus Guzm.-Dáv. & Guzmán (1986)
G. praecox (Peck) Murrill (1917)
G. praefloccosus Murrill (1941)
G. praelaeticolor Murrill (1945)
G. pratensis Singer (1952)
G. primulinus (Berk.) Pegler (1965)
G. psamminus (Berk.) Pegler (1988)
G. pseudocamerinus Singer (1951)
G. pseudofulgens Romagn. (1979)
G. pulchrifolius (Peck) Murrill (1917)
G. punctifolius (Peck) Singer (1951)
G. purpuratus (Cooke & Massee) Singer (1955)
G. purpureonitens (Cooke & Massee) Pegler (1965)

G. purpureosquamulosus Høil. (1998)
G. pusillus (Peck) Murrill (1917)
G. radicicola Singer (1977)
G. rigidus (Peck) Murrill (1917)
G. robustus Guzm.-Dáv. (1994)
G. rufescens Hesler (1969)
G. rufobrunneus Hesler (1969)
G. rufopunctatus (Pat. & Gaillard) Dennis (1970)
G. rufosquamulosus Hesler (1969)
G. rugulosus R. Valenz., Guzmán & J. Castillo (1981)
G. russipes Pegler (1983)
G. sapineus (Fr.) Murrill (1912)
G. satur Kühner
G. sordidostipes Hesler (1969)
G. spadiceus Romagn. (1977)
G. sphagnicola (Peck) Murrill (1917)
G. spinulifer Murrill
G. squalidus (Peck) Murrill (1917)
G. squamulose Murrill
G. stabilis (Weinm.) Kühner & Romagn. (1985)

G. subbellulus Hesler (1969)

G. subcarbonarius Murrill

G. subdryophilus Murrill (1940)

G. subearlei R. Valenz., Guzmán & J. Castillo (1981)

G. suberis (Maire) Singer (1951)

G. subflavidus Murrill

G. subfulgens Guzm.-Dáv. (1995)

G. subfulvus (Peck) Murrill (1917)

G. subgeminellus Guzm.-Dáv. & Guzmán (1986)

G. submarasmioides Singer (1977)

G. subpenetrans Murrill (1913)

G. subpurpuratus Guzm.-Dáv. & Guzmán (1991)

G. subrufobrunneus Guzm.-Dáv. & Guzmán (1986)

G. subsapineus Hesler (1969)

G. subspectabilis Hesler (1969)

G. subsphaerosporus (Joss.) Kühner & Romagn. (1953)

G. subtropicus Hesler (1969)

G. subviridis Murrill (1915)

G. tasmanicus B.J. Rees (1999)

G. tenuis Murrill (1943)

G. terrestris Hesler (1969)

G. terricola K.A. Thomas, Guzm.-Dáv. & Manim. (2003)

G. testaceus B.J. Rees (1999)

G. thiersii M.T. Seidl (1989)

G. tomentulosus B.J. Rees (1999)

G. tonkinensis (Pat.) Singer (1951)

G. trailii (Berk. & Cooke) Singer (1955)

G. tropicus Natarajan (1977)

G. turficola M. M. Moser & H. Ladurner (2008)[2]

G. tuxtlensis Guzm.-Dáv. (1994)

G. tyallus Grgur. (1997)

G. underwoodii (Peck) Murrill (1917)

G. unicolor Murrill

G. validipes (Peck) Hesler (1969)

G. velatus (Peck) Murrill (1917)

G. velutinus (Petch) Singer (1986)

G. ventricosus (Earle) Hesler (1969)

G. vialis Murrill

G. viridans Murrill

G. viscidissimus Murrill

G. viscidus (Peck) Murrill (1917)

G. weberi Murrill (1946)

G. yangshanensis Z.S. Bi (1990)

G. zempoalensis Guzmán & V. Mora (1984)

G. zenkeri (Henn.) Singer (1951)

Bibliography

Andersson, Christer, et al. *Occurrence and Use of Hallucinogenic Mushrooms Containing Psilocybin Alkaloids.* Nordic Council of Ministers, 2009.

Awan, Ali R., et al. "Convergent Evolution of Psilocybin Biosynthesis by Psychedelic Mushrooms." 2018, doi:10.1101/374199.

Berry, S. (2018). The incredible potential of magic mushrooms. *Microreviews in Cell and Molecular Biology, 4*(1).

Boer, Peter de. "Where Do Magic Mushrooms Grow? - Trufflemagic - Fresh Truffles & Grow Kits." *Trufflemagic,* 4 July 2017, www.trufflemagic.com/where-do-magic-mushrooms-grow/#Magic%20Mushrooms%20in%20Asia.

Brodwin, Erin. "Denver Just Became the First City in the US to Decriminalize Magic Mushrooms. Here's What They Do to Your Body and Mind." *Business Insider,* Business Insider, 9 May 2019, www.businessinsider.com/magic-mushrooms-psilocybin-mental-physical-effects-2019-5.

Cavanagh, Julien J., and Teresa Y. Smith. "Psychedelic Drug (LSD, PCP, Hallucinogenic Mushrooms) Intoxication." *Quick Guide to Psychiatric Emergencies,* 2017, pp. 199–203., doi:10.1007/978-3-319-58260-3_36.

Cockburn, Harry. "Wild Magic Mushrooms See Growth Bonanza in British Countryside after Mild Winter." *The Independent,* Independent Digital News and Media, 15 Jan. 2019, www.independent.co.uk/environment/magic-mushrooms-boom-england-warm-winter-climate-change-shropshire-staffordshire-drugs-a8728671.html.

Entheonation. "The Easy Guide On How To Identify Psilocybin Mushrooms." *EntheoNation,* entheonation.com/blog/psilocybin-mushrooms-identification/.

Feinberg, Benjamin. *The Devil's Book of Culture: History, Mushrooms, and Caves in Southern Mexico.* University of Texas Press, 2003.

Freeman, Shanna. "How Magic Mushrooms Work." *HowStuffWorks Science,* HowStuffWorks, 30 Aug. 2019, science.howstuffworks.com/magic-mushroom.htm.

Heinrich, Clark. *Magic Mushrooms in Religion and Alchemy.* Park Street Press, 2002.

Honyiglo, Emma, et al. "Unpredictable Behavior Under the Influence of 'Magic Mushrooms': A Case Report and Review of the Literature." *Journal of Forensic Sciences,* vol. 64, no. 4, 2018, pp. 1266–1270., doi:10.1111/1556-4029.13982.

Kuo, Daniel D., and Mau H. Kuo. *How to Grow Forest Mushroom (Shiitake) for Fun or Profit.* Mushroom Technology Corp., 1983.

Letcher, Andy. *Shroom: a Cultural History of the Magic Mushroom.* HarperCollins, 2008.

"Magic Mushrooms." *FRANK,* www.talktofrank.com/drug/magic-mushrooms#how-it-looks-tastes-and-smells.

Nicholas, L. G., and Kerry Ogame. *Psilocybin Mushroom Handbook: Easy Indoor and Outdoor Cultivation.* Quick American Archives, 2004.

Nutt, David. "Psilocybin for Anxiety and Depression in Cancer Care? Lessons from the Past and Prospects for the Future." *Journal of Psychopharmacology,* vol. 30, no. 12, 2016, pp. 1163–1164., doi:10.1177/0269881116675754.

O'hare, Ryan. "Can Psychedelic Drugs 'Reconnect' Depressed Patients with Their Emotions?" *Medical Xpress - Medical Research Advances and Health News,* Medical Xpress, 15 Jan. 2018, medicalxpress.com/news/2018-01-psychedelic-drugs-reconnect-depressed-patients.html.

Parsons, Haley. *Magic Mushrooms: Their Evolutionary History, Chemical Synthesis, and Pharmacological Use in Mood Disorders.* The Author, 2019.

Price, David, et al. "The Ultimate Guide to Psilocybin Mushrooms - Experience, Benefits, & Side Effects." *The Third Wave,* thethirdwave.co/psychedelics/shrooms/.

Ratti, Annie. *The Mushroom Project.* Roma Publications, 2014.

"Related Links." *EMCDDA,* www.emcdda.europa.eu/publications/drug-profiles/mushrooms.

Shiwnarain, Mohendra. "Magic Mushrooms Can Chemically 'Reset' A Depressed Brain." *Science Trends,* 2017, doi:10.31988/scitrends.3831.

Smith, Patrick. "Magic Mushroom Legality Around the World." *EntheoNation,* entheonation.com/blog/magic-mushroom-legality/.

Stafford, Peter G., and Jeremy Bigwood. *Psychedelics Encyclopedia.* Ronin Pub., 1992.

Stamets, Paul. *Psilocybin Mushrooms of the World: an Identification Guide.* Ten Speed Press, 1996.

Stamets, Paul. *Psilocybin Mushrooms of the World: an Identification Guide.* Ten Speed Press, 1996.

Tindale, Kathryn, and Lisa Steacy. "Councillor Wants to Halt Plans for a Magic Mushroom Dispensary in Vancouver." *NEWS 1130,* 22 July 2019.